SECUNDUM IPSUM

or

THE MAGISTER LIBELLUS

"I have been cozened and bejaped," quoth he gruffly.

— The White Company

To all of the children who awaken prematurely, to those who look forward to a lifetime of karmic struggle, and to those who may ultimately succeed – I love you and I wish you the greatest expediency in a dawning sunrise.

"There is no work honestly finished, except as it is abandoned by its creator. All things are in a state of becoming, and so, as this manuscript has been in formation for several millennia, I offer to you, my reader, this newest translation and re-edited interpretation. It is in no way complete, nor should it be. Countless numbers will follow, and so this is not the first edition, nor the last."

— Fra.E.E., The Corpus Hermeticum.

The Birth of Faith

Aima's silver fur rippled with waves of yellow confusion and orange discomfort. The voices told her that he was her soul mate; her light, her life, her love. Those same voices told her that he'd abandoned her before.

She anchored herself near to where her body relaxed on the floor and paid it little attention, "It's only meat." She announced to no one in particular.

A cool golden-blue shape flittered past her, tickling Aima's aura with a wave of giddy excitement, but still it would not speak with her. Aima had only become aware of its presence two months ago, and named it Faith.

"You have to admit, Aima, that "Love" is not a powerful enough word to describe this sensation. We are magickians, and of the Children of the Light, no less. People fear what we are capable of. People crave what we are capable of." Ego Esse explained.

This man, this human, this animal body, its voice just an echo of its true vibration, was so much more on the Astral-Plane than was seen on the Physical. His form here was a myriad of geometrical shapes, spinning within and orbiting around each other, sparks of colorful aetheric light shooting out of his centers like so many stars in a galaxy. There were few like him – a fumbling, stuttering creature physically, a glittering, glowing Flower of Life on the Astral.

The sensation he was describing was so much more than meat-puppet humans called "Love". Indeed, it manifested itself in their physical realities as tantric orgasms delivered at a distance of twenty miles; they had touched each others bodies with their minds, and the results were staggering.

When she met him, he was a pathetic genius, with a talent for dramatics and a flair for the tantric-quabalah. Most would call it magick. She was becoming Buddhistically aware – enlightened in a way that few humans could comprehend. Faith was the distillation of that emotion, their unborn, non-corporeal daughter.

"But", she thought, "he has left me before. Hundreds, thousands of lifetimes, each one different, and mysteriously, this remains the same." Millions of years of shared loneliness consumed her, blanketing her fur in a solid orange glow.

"You're silly, Mommy." Faith giggled, but though she could see her and feel her, Aima still could not hear her.

"Faith is our belief. She is our religion. She is our symbol of a divine union. If you like, she is our savior. Stop this nonsense about my leaving again. I am in you and all around you." Ego Esse's aura grew, enveloping both Aima's and Faith's forms in a broad, pink and white glow.

In the bed below them, Ego Esse and Aima joined, their bodies concentrated, their souls fused above and below them, the golden-blue orb finding solace in the physical womb, nestling comfortably in the zygote created by this marriage of souls. "I do", she whispered, "My everything."

Dialogue

"All evil genius' are writers. Quite simply, in order to become a successful villain, you must have a challenge to overcome, and thus is created your plot. As any true villain is a person with the ability to justify their actions, they are also quite egotistical and obsessive – this is often the curse of the evil genius, and so he becomes his own protagonist. This is also the curse of the amateur writer."

"I read somewhere that artists are usually quite mad. They see the world in ways different than most people. They experience life in the creative state of mind, that is, in the imagination. They share this reality with those people they come into contact with. They expect these people to see their world, knowing that it is not a shared reality. In psychological circles, this is called schizophrenia. Often, I am told, the same quote recurs from writers, musicians, and painters, "I want to induce a particular emotional state in my audience. I want them to see through my eyes, hear through my ears, to know what I know, to feel what I feel." Art, I suppose, is a form of sociopathic manipulation."

"No, Art is therapy. Therapy removes fear. Fear is usually induced by an overactive imagination. Art is induced by overactive imaginations as a balancing factor. The best therapy is erasure – not disclosure. Remove the art from the artist, and you are left with a person who stares blankly at a coloring book. Remove the fear from the patient, and you are left with a person who stares blankly at a poisonous spider."

"Really? Happy endings are called both comedies and tragedies. Both end with "Happily Ever After". If not a comedy, then a tragedy, or what is commonly referred to as a fable. Fairie Tales or Fables? Happy sugar coated endings, or morals and ethical lessons. Consider a comical tragedy? Or a tragical comedy? It breaks the rules, at least in as much as the good guy is also the

9

bad guy. Othello, Dracula, and where reality follows art, so too was Aleister Crowley. Each and every person is their own worst enemy, in that he or she is their own source of suffering. People are wired for self-destruction. We anchor onto negative emotions, and become addicted to a certain chemical mix of endorphins. You show me a human being, and I will show you a totally predictable personality structure."

"An arch-villain must have his own auto-destruct, and the protagonist is also the hero, at least in as much as the audience is supposed to identify themselves with them. All hero's eventually burn out. Far too often it is the villain that treats his children well. Hero's all too often ignore their progeny."

A Letter

Cara Frater,   25 Adar I 5763

"The circle is the two dimensional shadow of the sphere which is regarded throughout cultural history as an icon of the ineffable oneness; the indivisible fulfillment of the universe. All other symbols and geometries reflect various aspects of the profound and consummate perfection of the circle, sphere and other higher dimensional forms of these we might imagine." – Sacred Geometry

Imagine in your minds eye opening the kitchen door and discovering everything missing. In their places, you find a series of numerical equivalents, a line here, a platonic solid there. Instinctively, if you are of a scientific mind like my own, you will see the numbers near the lines, a diagram and schematic of the universe above your electric conventional oven. Perhaps if you are unused to such phenomenon occurring in your universe, you would calmly shake your head, exit the room, and calmly call your psychiatrist. Not I, as this is my usual experience of the universe. See as well the etheric fields surrounding objects. Some would call this the astral plane. My closest friends call it schizophrenic experience. Think of it as you might a person with x-ray vision, except instead of bones he is looking at your mind, your soul. It is a kind of radiation both within you and without you. It is as if you were transparent and I could see the energy fields around you, behind you, inside you. Strange geometrical shapes in your aura, star tetrahedrons, spheres, and spinning magnetic fields. The Vedas calls them Chakras. The Kabbalah calls them Sephirot. To understand the mind of the magickian is to consider the filters through which he or she experiences the universe without him. Each and every human being filters the true universe through his beliefs, through his experience, and through his assumptions. The magickian does not have to carry any beliefs, does not carry assumptions, and considers the experience fallible. "I have come

11

to believe that the whole world is an enigma that is made terrible by our own mad attempt to interpret it as though it had an underlying truth." – Umberto Eco

In Lvx,
Frater Chesed, Societas De Angilluminatus

888

The Earth is dying. After a hundred and fifty years of Industrial damage and exploitation, we have finally signed our planet's death warrant, and carried out her execution. There was no call to stay by the governor, who, as representative of the people endorsed rather than dissuaded the action.

With no other choice but to count down the hours, cough until we choke, or otherwise wait for a miracle, a plan was hatched. Its chances of success were drastically minimal, as human calculation could only take for granted those things we did not know, such as whether or not the planet would recreate life or simply die. Our hope was on the Earth restablizing its already critical condition.

There was a group of Christian Scientists who did not believe that salvation was a possibility, letting their twisted idea of Faith desiccate their attempts at saving our dying planet. It was the common Christian belief that not only was this execution foretold in the Book of Revelations, but that we were not to save ourselves. To do so would be sin. Who would have known that halting the extinction of our race would also be justification for losing our souls?

Who knew how our idea would work out? Every country for itself. America was doomed from the start. The only thing that bureaucrats could decide upon was to hide the warden's underground and hope that no one else survived to observe their cowardice.
Only the strongest survive. Nope. The strongest were too busy with last minute preparations that they could not take the least of actions towards healing the planet. The most inventive? Perhaps, but even they were still too uncivilized to realize that doom was upon them.

The Canadians shrugged, awaiting doomsday with an observed indifference. When the Prime-Minister was asked what his country was doing, he replied, "We tried Kyoto. We tried clean energy. We tried passing laws and making amendments to laws. Our closest neighbors were not willing to follow our lead, and so, our efforts have been in vain." He went to the Caribbean, political consultant in tow, and left the actors in charge of government. Who better to run the show? Got more done, too, with all the scheduled intrigue and gossip to make it all worth televising.

I was in Spain when the siren called my name. She was the most beautiful woman I'd ever seen. It was not a practical beauty that most men would find attractive. She was subtle, but her genuine intelligence flowed through her like the energy of a Baptist choir. She moved gracefully, stepping to a song that no one else could hear. Her blonde hair was cut short and feathered about her face, and her slender fingers ended in well kept nails which only secretaries and actresses could hope to produce. Her eyes were too large for her face, a very unattractive feature to most, but she would burst into poetic song at the drop of a hat, chanting the most romantic Byron or Shelley to any listening ear.

"Amanda", I answered, shocked that I would meet her so far from home. "What in God's unholy names are you doing here?"

"Enjoying my last days. My Gods, you look different. I almost didn't recognize you. She referred to my hair, which was usually worn long and black, and was now cut short and dyed an orange-red.

"You are still a goddess", I replied, burying my face in her hair as I picked her up from the street, spinning her in a tight hug. I had last seen Amanda in Canada, where we worked together at a psychic consultation firm.

We spent the next three hours in a pub, drinking espresso and reminiscing. When we had finished, the bells rang for nine o'clock curfew and we separated with a kiss long in the coming.

Having exchanged cellular numbers and hotel addresses, I assured myself that nothing was coincidental, and we should soon meet again.

The International News Service broadcasted a breaking article on the newest wave of technological "earthsavers", designed to reincarnate our devastated planet after the disaster's worst had passed. Somehow, despite mankind's apocalyptic efforts to save what was left of ourselves, the corporate standard of supply and demand can still produce a profit from the last days.

Construction had been completed on seven huge superstructures, designed by the *** Corporation to house the frozen corpses of one hundred thousand people, as well as enough food and water for a five year span. The libraries within the time capsule contained the complete knowledge of mankind, down to sealed files of the governments of the world. Naught would be lost, and the corporation promised to reseed the planet with its form of Genesis immediately following the world's restabalization.

The first of the two structures could be found in Nepal, and was already selling front row tickets to the New World. I was very intrigued that the very rich were denied access, as were government officials. All participants were thoroughly identified with advanced DNA tests, along with the standard methods of screening. The second superstructure was located in Canada, near the lea of the Columbia Mountains. I had never understood the reasoning behind their choices of location, and indeed, never got an answer. The third was built in Jerusalem, and others in Peru, Australia, Scandanavia, and Switzerland.

I thought it interesting that none of the great Pyramidal structures were built in the United States, and the *** Corporation was unwilling to release its methods to any government. A public statement was made to the associated press that "Government figures are often unstable in their knowledge and irresponsible with their logic."

The *** Corporation was in fact the only real company with any real ability to produce the results it claimed. Its employees were not paid in cash, but in company credit and education. They were given everything they asked, and worked towards the salvation of the planet and the human race. The worlds greatest scientists were among their staff, and none among them would speak of their commitment, except that it was lucrative.

The churches believed that the *** Corporation was a multinational corporate cult, whose members were brainwashed into selling their souls in trade for immortality and worldly comforts.

The New Agers and conspiracy theorists believed that the *** Corporation were led by an alien race who were playing on mankind's fears of obliteration sought a slave race who's population could be managed and controlled.

Everyone in the "civilized world", if it could be called such, were aware that through irresponsibility we had conceived the end of the world. Pollution, war, the Ozone hole, Global warming, &c. had all taken their toll. Scientists estimated ten years before the planet would become too hot to support life. The oceans, some said, would boil in near a decade's time. Others soon found that the estimates were wrong, and that the Global Warming trend created exponential damage, not cumulative.

In the last year of the second millennium, the Earth's average temperature had risen by two degrees Celsius and that in four years it would have risen an average of four degrees, and in ten years, eight degrees, and by the end of the second decade, not even the cockroaches would have a place to hide.

They were wrong, of course. We had only three years. The summer storms and monsoons raged, inland hurricanes thrashed the fields and warnings were often declared hours too late. Humanity, and her planet, were doomed.

Many people cashed in their chips, but most tried their best to ignore the impending doom. I went to the country, and then traveled. I ran into Amanda in Rome, and then continued our travels together, deciding that if the world will die, we would see as much of it as we could together before we died too.

We backpacked through Europe for six months, and were married in a small village in France. We rented a car in Berlin, which somehow never seemed to get returned, and eventually found ourselves in India. Six months more passed, and we stayed as far away from the major storms of the world, but the worst had only begun. The forests of India had succumbed to the ever increasing heat, and the mountain glaciers had melted, causing landslides and devastating floods. Crops had failed the world over – whether through flooding or drought.

"There is something I have to tell you." Amanda began. We were holed up for three days in an Indian hotel room, basking in air conditioned glory. Now was a better time than never.

"Oh, yeah? What's that?"

"We have tickets for the Ark in Calgary."

"That's insane!" I exclaimed, temperature rising to meet the already overworked air conditioner. I wanted to be angry with her, but knew that it would devastate her. She had shown me a side of herself that I had never expected to see. We often laughed and mocked with a wonderful sarcasm both the Ark Project as well as the religious opposition that it received. Somehow I didn't really think about the great pyramids of human salvation, and sort of hoped I'd pass on with a bang. Amanda, despite being very unconventional, seemed to become the more responsible.

I hugged her and told her that I wasn't angry with her, and she cried when I said, "I love you so, I will live for you."

We caught the first airship to Canada and found a ready transport waiting for us in Toronto. We were greeted at the airport by one of the ***'s officials.

"So, you aren't going to cut off our heads and freeze them in liquid nitrogen, are you?" I asked him jovially.

"Yeah, cause I'd hate to give up my tattoo, I doubt it'd show up on the cloned body you'd give me." Amanda added, feign seriousness glowing from her beautiful face.

The official looked at us with a shock of uncertainty on his face, and then realized with a chuckle that we were pulling his leg. A man nearby offered that cloning was illegal in the United States, but was sure that the president had it done for him before election time.

The jet was boarded and we were pleased to discover that it had air conditioning. Amanda continued to stare at the other passengers, starting brief conversations with some, and ending conversations with others.

We were flown to Winnipeg and told that there was to be a short stopover before continuing to Calgary. I had not been back in Canada in nearly four years, and the cities had become metropolis monstrosities since I'd last been there. The downtown core of

Calgary had grown from a small handful of skyscrapers and a population of just over one million to four hundred square miles of concrete and steel superstructures housing over one hundred million refugees.

Our official had us immediately board a bus directly from the plane to save time, as we were to be in hibernation within the hour.

888 Atziluth Drive, built on what used to be the largest shopping mall in North America. Somehow it suited us. The view was surrealistic. An eighty story pyramid, fashioned of concrete with an inch thick titanium shell. Near the top of the monument was a six story tall Udjat – an Egyptian Eye of Horus, black obsidian bricks inset into the titanium coating.

"Novus Ordo Seclorum." I said in a near whisper. Amanda replied "Annuit Coeptis."

The heat was almost unbearable as we got out of the transport. The dry wind whipped us as the sun disappeared behind the pyramid sending a halo of rays to either side of the point, the sixty foot tall eye staring down at us.

The crowd rushed towards the entrance, two large titanium doors at the base of the outer temple – the shadow of the pyramid offering little relief from the terrible heat.

As Amanda and I approached, an usher handed us two small plastic bracelets, the UPC barcodes glowing against the white wristband. "The New World Order. Where's my gold star? They might as well know I'm Jewish, too." Amanda giggled, gripped my hand tighter and kissed my cheek.

"And I will give him the morning star ", she said. "Or something like this: 'And he causeth all to receive a mark of the name of the beast and the number of its name.'"

I laughed, and an elderly woman gave us a fearful look before grasping her bag to her chest and hurrying towards the doors. Yelling, we chanted, "Let he who hath understanding reckon the number of the beast, for it is a human number, and its number is six hundred and sixty six..."

"Plus two twenty two!" I cried as we fell to the earth, rolling upon the ground in fits of laughter, our blasphemy completed.

When our display of humor subsided, we shook ourselves off and continued on towards the door. Upon our arrival, our names were taken, our belongings searched for perishables, and our information recorded, including our wristbands.

We were lead into a large chamber, where we were fed a blue pill, which was intended to slow our metabolisms in preparation for hibernation. Amanda smiled as we were lead again down a corridor large enough to drive a train through, if one were compelled to do such a thing.

Into a room we were taken, where we sat down upon the concrete floor. A crowd was gathered there around us. They were talking, and all seemed quite excited about the entire ordeal. A young man with wavy blonde hair was showing his friend a magazine with his picture in it. Another was boring his wife with the details of the hibernation process. One young woman was exclaiming that all of us were going to die in the pyramid, but that it was okay with her. She explained to any who would listen that she was going to die on her own terms, and began to remove her clothing.

The room was slowly filling to capacity, and a disembodied voice explained that all were to sit or lay down on the floor as the doors were closed and the room pressurized. Amanda was startled by a child's plea for help, and a little boy was drawn to us by a young blonde girl. " He's lost his mom", she explained, and Amanda tried to calm the child down.

Somehow, I had never seen the maternal nature in her before, always so full of our shared bohemian attitude that I never had the opportunity. "It's okay, it will be okay. You can stay with us for now. Come, sit with me." The little boy calmed immediately and I wiped the tears from his face with a silk kerchief. "What is your name? I am Amanda, this is Lucidus."

"Freedom" the boy replied, tears still in his voice.

"Well, Freedom, you'll be okay with us. Come, sit down. The boy smiled and curled up in my lap, his blonde head leaning against my shoulder as he fell asleep. Amanda held my hand and we curled up against the corner as the other sat and laid down on the cold concrete floor.

"Embrionic   Phase   will   proceed   in   ten seconds…nine…eight…seven…" The door to the room was closed and sealed. I felt the same sort of exhilaration that often overcomes people with the take off of a jet plane. "…five…four…" I could hear a faint hissing sound from the ceiling of the room. I kissed Amanda, and the child Freedom, murmuring, "I'll see you on the other side."

The room seemed cold as I watched people begin nodding off. One by one I watched as their breathing ceased and their chests stopped moving. The fruity smell became stronger, and Amanda's hold on my hand grew tight as I realized that she too was no longer breathing. The child lay still in my lap. I looked around the room, noting the pert brown nipples of the young woman who insisted upon dying on her own terms, and the young man with his magazine article. Somehow, my world froze, and there was no more.

Angillumintus

He grew up blind. His entire life, blindness meant to him that he would never know racism. Blindness meant to him that he could see past simple imperfections, and deeper into the heart and soul of those he spoke to.

Well practiced was he in his ability to listen, to respond in kindness, and to devote every second of attention to being a passionate audience. These traits had two particular effects on people. No matter their background, no matter their race, no matter their religion, no matter their memberships or affiliations, no matter their state or mind or level of education, he made them feel important, appreciated and loved. No matter how insignificant their words, no matter how unimportant their opinion, he made them feel intelligent, if only for a brief space of time.

Most people in passing did not realize that he lived in a world of blindness. Those who knew him only recognized his talent for communicating, and how he made them feel important.

When she met him the second time, she did not recognize him. Six months before they had met, and a brief conversation imprinted his voice into her mind. At that time, both recognized an instant connection, a chemistry, the promise of Love. He was not struck by her pretty face or her athletic form. He was unmoved by her white teeth or her blonde hair. These he couldn't see for her. He saw in her the one thing that never effected to attract a man before. He saw her as she truly was. The only description he could give was "Light". In a world of darkness, she was the light. At once he could see. Not in the miraculous manner of the Fountain at Lourdes, nor even in the typically secular concept of sunlight on the retina. She was, and is, his Light: Shekhina!

A further six months later they met again. Though they did not recognize each other, on a subtle unconscious level, they knew. When he spoke in her presence, she was struck in awe by his grace and magnetic charm. She must make contact with him, but like most men felt when confronted with her beauty, she did not know how to approach him.

He did not know her, and could not perceive her except as another body in the crowd which jostled and brushed past him. He did not hear her when she spoke, as she was only one of the hundreds of voices that rang out in the air about him. Suddenly, a light: Blue; showering him, filling him, enveloping him. He knew the sensation – Attraction – Arousal – Affection – Appreciation – Anticipation. A pentalpha, the five pointed star equating only to the Eternal Triunity of Love:

JEHESHUAH!

And the light sparked his emotion like no other could. He could see it surrounding his form like a plasma – he could sense an outline against the darkness – and like the first eruption of consciousness, he understood:

I AM! I EXIST! EHEIEH!

They spent a thousand years together in the brief space of a month. Every moment amplified by their perfect attentiveness. They were inseparable, and he did not know jealousy in her presence as one of those with eyes for such would. He knew how others wanted her, but also knew that she too had become blind.

In her, he learned to see beauty. In him, she closed her eyes to the emotional corruption that often obscures the mind. Some say, and quite accurately in most respects, that Love is blind. Others – again, accurately and often without circumstantial bias – that ignorance is bliss. She taught him to see, as if for the first time, the colors right there in front of him: Glossy ochres, dull pearl shades of white and black, viridian hues of green, sharp tones of red. She showed him a life he had never before experienced. He showed her how to hear, how to listen, and how to appreciate subtle nuances in inflection.

He was not physically incapable of vision, just as she was not physically incapable of sound. The two, they became one, and in respect to the gifts they shared, taught the blind to see and the deaf to hear. Is this love? Neither knew the word. This is more than passion, though neither could express it as such. It was in fact both on a higher octave, as only Gods know — and these two may share it with the world.

Those who have Ears to hear, let them hear!
Those who have Eyes to see, let hem see!
SPIRIT OF THE EARTH, REMEMBER!
SPIRIT OF THE SKY, REMEMBER!

Discorsi Mystica

Mysticism, the belief and the pursuit of the unification of the Divine Principle. The gnosis of divine truth. The direct experience of Internal Divinity. This is the true Catholic Science, which unites all religions within the true religion of God, which knows no doctrine or dogma – the quest for divinity.

If you were to search for Christ, that is, messianic consciousness, without ever knowing the bible or its laws, without ever hearing an idolatrous word spoken in the name or the blood of god, would the same divine being hear you? Is God undifferentiated? What name would you assign to IT? The name of a thing implies the relationship with that thing. The thought is implied by the word, and thus the word, no matter what its shape, is enclothed with the same meaning. This domain of esoteric discipline, called occult by the less informed, becomes the known unknown. It is the heart of philosophy.

To close the lips and eyes (Myein) is the secret oath of the ancient initiate, the Mystes. The sign of silence, the finger held softly, but firm over the lip, to keep most secret the inner workings of the temple. The application of awareness over ignorance.

Mysticism is the awareness of the secrets of the mind, and is the true occultism. There is a danger there, which is subtle, and undermines even the most disciplined. The astute scholar will know this sign, the sign of obscurity over the eyes, a blanket over the awareness. The blindness which occurs only to those who have accepted falsity. The true mystic will seek the light, to remove the veil, and accept only what is true, what is verifiable within direct experience. There are no magical powers, no mystical events which do occur outside of natural occurrence. Even those effects of the mind upon the material body work within particular laws. There are no mysteries in the universe which the mind of man cannot discern – including the mysteries of God.

Mysticism is not the same to every person experiencing gnosis. To many, the inspiration is entirely academic and scientific – the philosophical impressions may read like a text book. To another, the gnosis is accompanied by a powerful euphoric sensation. To yet another, it may be accompanied by visions, sensations, and hallucinations. One certainty is clear, in whatever form the experience takes – it must be verifiable to be thought of as real. To speak in a language without knowing its meaning and expecting another to call it the "Language of the Fowels" or the "Greene Tongue" will do no good unless the interpretation is clear to those who speak the language fluently. Scribbling upon a sheet of paper is nonsense unless it is legible to the intelligent observer. A theory which is gleaned from the divine ethers may be inspired, but can only be considered accurate if they are true within the realms of scientific inquiry. If a theory is shown to be inaccurate, it must be discarded as worthless, or at least modified to conform to acceptable standards of logical thought.

Within the divine principle, there are two forms: he who seeks after unity and identity with the universal principle, and he who seeks after unity and identity with God. The Divine principle is best described in the term "Thou art God", and is often found within the ideology of Taoism – interconnectedness and oneness with the All. It is the "I Am" of Divine inspiration. It can be experienced through meditation and constant awareness – the invocation of the eternal and absolute Be-ing.

Unity and identity with God – that is, the most divine and indefinable aspect of God that is beyond all interpretation or explanation – is found in all religious systems, though not necessarily in their most public forms. These forms often assume the symbolic structures of the beliefs and practices of the practitioners, which often affects objectivity through the corrupted lens of pretext. Symbols within a religious system are defined by their associations to mythological significance, and objectivity will only be possible within strict limitations of that system. This becomes a mystical communion with the sacred within that particular belief system, and thus becomes segregated from any other by its bias (for example, the symbol of the pentacle may be discerned as a beautiful and powerful symbol in one instance, and a destructive and terrible symbol in another).

Absolute Natural Mysticism is unaffected by an imposed pretext, and is only defined by a natural relationship to its environment. All boundaries between the subject and the object is obliterated, and pure gnosis is attained. It is a knowledge which is entirely abstract, but may be described in logical terms. The pentagram is thus discovered within the apple core, the golden mean is found within the canon of man, and the shape of chaos is found to have structure after all.

Hermionicon

When you come to the edge of all the light you have, and you must step into the darkness of the unknown, either there will be something solid for you to stand on, or you will fall.

Wisdom cannot be a thing conquered, and if sought, it may not be found. There are no truths in the universe, except the truths we make for ourselves. There are no right answers, there are only assumptions, impressions, theories, opinions, and suggestions – but truth is a generalization.

We must ignore all that we have previously believed. We must demonstrate a kind of erasure of "knowledge". The only truth available to mankind is found in silence. True and total silence, of both the body and of the mind. It is the very rare individual who can truly state the most profound truth, "I don't know."

We cannot be seduced by the deception of knowledge. There is no history except as our mind makes it so.

Each and every person lives in a state of past experience. All new sensations we receive are seconds old before we are able to act on them, and often several more seconds pass before we make a decision to act.

Each mind is trained through classical conditioning to accept certain actions and behaviors as a natural default. It is our intention to destroy these patterns of behavior and make every decision by the moment rather than by the programmed response.

Every person is capable of perfection. "Every man and every woman is a star" and the realization of this is the realization of one's own divinity.

There are no abstractions except the beliefs that we choose to subscribe to. Limiting these beliefs to a complete understanding of reality as it presents itself cannot be explained by words, and judgments should not be made.

Magic is the willingness to make a goal and pursue it to its completion. Meditation is the training of the mind and of the body. There are psychical developments which occur as side effects to these practices, such as the controlled creation of hallucination, telepathy, and clairvoyance, but these are only signposts that indicate one's degree of performance. They are not goals in and of themselves.

Truth is only found in silence. Truth is assumption that your theory is accurate. Truth, as it is commonly understood, is the belief in a psychological model of reality that we each make up in our own minds to explain the universe described by our senses. It is an imperfect representation, using imperfect senses, and limited further by our biological and psychological imperfections.

Truth is the acceptance of a theoretical model of the universe. This is the first secret of awareness, that reality is entirely mental. Each idea is a symbol, made relevant by our associations with it. Each object, each experience is defined by our interaction with it, but it has no reality but that which we give to it.

Formulae of the Cult
(Modified from the original text.)

I. We undertook this grand endeavor, and promised to you, beloved, to treat of that grace and truth, and to show how, as a matter belonging to the Highest Order, as it is to be distinguished from the rest. Give, then, your attention that what I receive in my measure, you may in your measure receive and hear the same. For it will only remain if, when the disincarnate seed is scattered in your hearts, the thorns of ignorance will not choke it, nor will the heat of material lust scorch it, and there will descend upon it the rain of daily exhortations and your own purified thoughts, by which that is done in the heart which in the field is done by means of harrows, so that the clod is broken, and the seed covered and enabled to germinate: that you will bear the fruit of a purified mind.

2. I do not think that I need spend much time in endeavoring to persuade you that we are more than merely human; and if mere humans, by virtue of the species, we have become more so. Upon the forehead we bear the sign of the Mark; and we must keep silence because of it, for we also bear it also in the heart. His sign is the proof of our agency. By a star the Magi knew Christ; by diverse miracles did the sages know Buddha, and this sign was given by the Illuminated to us. The initiates which precede us desire that a star should be his sign on the forehead of the faithful. By it we are humbled, and by it we are also glorified; by it we raise the dead, even by that to which we may, when challenged, cast down the living. We belong, then, to ourselves, we belong to the Divine. "The law was given by Moses, but grace and truth came only by God." We ask only divine inspiration to become more than we are, since we are not under the law but under truth. Behold, for this end have we come, that we might redeem ourselves from under the law; that now we may not be under the law, but under the guidance of true gnosis and the

governance of perfect wisdom. Why are we not subject to the laws of man? It is not justification for ignorance, for true wisdom is never above another. The laws of man are in place for the purpose of man's governance, but we live in accordance to another law, a higher purpose. There is no need for written laws when we have no reason to challenge them. The higher law is perfection of self, and in this, the old laws become obsolete. They are the control machine of animals, we belong to a higher jurisdiction.

3. The cure to all wounds is within you, hidden in the bandages of your own mind. There you are healed of Death eternal through many methods, if you choose to deny temporal death, or to move through it. And in this teaching does death die. What death was that, which slew death!

4. "In the beginning was the Word." In what beginning? "And the Word was with God." And what Word? "And the Word was God." Was then perhaps this Word made by God? No. For, "the same was in the beginning with God." There is a certain Illumination within mankind: let us see how lower man differs from the higher man, and then we shall understand what the light of gnosis is: you do not differ from the common man except in intellect, and wisdom; do not glory in anything besides. Common man lives in a state of illusion and obscuration. The "Word" is a silent one, and can only be attained in silence, and the discourse of silence will dispel the illusion as well. Do you presume upon your own strength? The wild beasts will overpower you. Do you presume upon your own swiftness? The flies that feast on corpses will overcome you. Do you presume upon physical beauty? The peacock has overwhelmed you with a feather. How then are you greater than them? Because you are made in the "Image of God?" What image: two arms, two legs, torso and head? Then monkey too has the image. Where is the image? The mind of man is what separates it from beast, in a most rare and uncertain measure. It is mankind's intellect; the light of men is the light of the mind. The

light of the mind is above the minds of the creatures of the earth, it is above the minds of the creatures of the water, and it is above the minds of the creatures of the air, for it also surpasses all minds of mankind if cultivated so. This was the Light by which all things were made.

5. If mankind holds the lantern within the mind, why is it not seen? Because "the light shines in darkness, and the darkness comprehends it not." Oh men, be not darkness, be not unbelieving, unjust, unrighteous, rapacious, avaricious lovers of this world: for these are the darkness. The light is not absent, but you are absent from the light. A blind man in the sunshine has the sun present to him, but is himself absent from the sun. "We are sometimes in darkness, but still light the world with our being." "What is the true Light which enlightens every man that comes into the world?" Because then the light of men was not seen, that is, the Light of the Mind, one who is not in darkness, but who is already enlightened; but because enlightened, not the light itself, for, "he was not that light." And what was the light? As the light of the sun, of the moon, and of lamps, was that light thus in the world? No. Because "the world was made by the Word, and the world does not know it;" that is to say, "the light shines in darkness, and the darkness comprehends it not." For the world is darkness; because the lovers of the world are the world. For did not the creature acknowledge its Creator? The heavens gave testimony by the stars; the sea gives testimony, by bearing a reflection; the winds gave testimony, and bear the bow across the firmament; the earth gave testimony, and in its glass and gems becomes enamored with the Light. If all these gave testimony, in what sense did the world not know Him, unless that the world signifies the lovers of the world, those who with their hearts dwell in the world? And the world is dark, because the inhabitants of the world are ignorant.

6. To those who dwell within this Light, to them is given power to become the Beni Elohim, the Sons of God." If they become

sons, they are born; if born, how are they born? Not of flesh, nor of blood, nor of the will of the flesh, nor of the will of man, but of the mind they are born, and this is the Mark upon the forehead that we bear as the symbol of the covenant. "And the Word became flesh, and dwelt among us." If the Word was not ashamed to be born of man, are men ashamed to be born of God? The Mind becomes a medicine to us, so that as by earth we were made blind, by earth we might be healed; and having been healed, might behold what? "And we beheld the glory of the true mind, full of grace and truth."

7. Listen to the voice of the mind, of the Light: "Before Lucifer I have begotten Thee." He who was begotten before Lucifer Himself illuminates all. It is said that a certain being was named Lucifer, who fell; for he was an angel and became a devil; "Lucifer, who did arise in the morning, fell" And why was he Lucifer, the morning and the evening star? Because, being enlightened, he gave forth light. But for what reason did he become dark! Because he abode not in the truth? No, because discovering that Truth in dialogue was eventually proven false, and he became silent: as the light arises in the morning and sets in the evening, does it not arise again the following day? In Silence is the Word. Therefore, before Lucifer, before every one that is enlightened; of necessity He must be, by whom all are enlightened who can be enlightened.

8. Let not each one flatter himself, but let him return into his own conscience, seek out the secret places of his own thoughts, recall the series of his deeds; let him not consider what he is if now he is something, but what he was that he might be something: he will find that he was not worthy of anything save life or death. If, then, you were worthy of death, of light extinguished, are you no better off than any other man who resides in darkness? There is no sin greater than ignorance. There is no law which governs the wise, for the wise are the Light by which the law is read. There is no "sin" except ignorance. There

is no punishment for this sin except continued existence in darkness.

9. If darkness was due, darkness was given, not light bestowed; but if it was light due, you were enlightened; but if, as is true, you were ignorant, consider by what right hangs over you by the law, and what you have obtained by mind. But having obtained that grace of illumination, you shall not seek justification for unlawful action, for you have set as the sun. Become silent, and set upon the wisdom which is within – there you will find the essence of your trouble, and seek to resolve it. It is in this way that your light will transcend that of mankind, and shall receive immortality as a reward, and life eternal. Life is not of flesh and bone, but of mind which transcends the body. The ignorant have memory swept away, the enlightened remember from life to life.

10. "Who was before a blasphemer, and a persecutor, and injurious; but I obtained light through the mind, and only in silence is the truth found." There are no extraneous offers here, but verifiable proof through practice. Do the obese believe that through exercise they will become healthy? No, for they must justify their sloth and feed their fears. It is only those who act in the light of knowledge and believe in the fruit of their labors who obtain the goal they seek. Just so, I can compose the path towards light in written form while remaining in silence, and you will not see it until you experience it. The light does not come as proof before the work, but only as a result of work. Leave the dogs to the dogs and do what thou wilt. Truth for Truth;" that is, for through this silence by which we live we shall receive another truth. What, then, is it except illumination? For if I shall say that this also is true, I attribute something to myself as if to me it were true. But we are crowned only by our own silence; but on condition that we walk with perseverance and surpass the simple-minded practices of our less significant brothers.

11. "For the law was given by Moses". Which law held the guilty? The law entered that the offense might be found. It was of benefit to the proud that the offense itself flourished, for they gave much to themselves, attributing strength to their own strength; but the lawgivers are unable to find truth.

12. If, then, there is one wanting to find the truth in silence, why does he not practice the meditations which lead to illumination? Because born with the heritage of ignorance, and taught nothing but circuitous inquiry since birth, finds no truth in the studies of mankind. He draws incomplete conclusions and arguments with him, convinced that they are complete and true, regardless of the loose logic with which they were founded, and are ceaselessly confounded.

The first man felt, and all who were born of him from him derived the desires of the flesh. It becomes unusual that another man should be born who derived no desire for the earthly world, who saw that there was no completion in works of the flesh. A man and a man: a man to death and a man to life. Thus saith the initiated: "Man may, indeed, choose ignorance and death, by the same seed, man may also choose illumination and awareness beyond death and death and death again." Men are not compelled towards awareness: because man's material nature is towards comfort. It is those who experience the divine union through their own inward illumination that attain to higher knowledge, the gnosis which is the seed disincarnate. To seek after knowledge requires the understanding that one is not comfortable, and the discomfort must overwhelm immobility. It is through quietude and separation that mankind may seek after the hidden knowledge, and remove the blindfold from the eyes.

13. Death is the natural punishment of ignorance, but if it is a natural accompaniment, then it is not punishment, but an effect of a cause. Subsequently, eternal existence is not a reward measured for those deserving few, but is a natural reaction to developing oneself. There is no outcry from the lesser mortals, for

they cannot conceive of such a truth. For them is only pain and death, law and punishment, ignorance and blindness. They do not see what is before them, and mock if they are presented it. It is realized through the journey, and without the calcinating fires of experience there is no awareness, no light, and no illumination. "Behold, the Prince of this World cometh, the Morning and the Evening Star, and he finds nothing in me." He had not in Himself any reason why He should die, and He died: his body did not move, was cold, an empty vessel. But one did come who bore the same mind, and in that coming showed the truth of illumination. There is no death but for those of limited mind. Light and Life are the same. So rare are these, and silence has overcome their tongue, so that they will not share their gnosis with the unready. The truth is in action, and action is in silence. An illuminated man is still a human being, but moreso. The lower nature having been consumed by the fires of enlightenment, caution is taken in all affairs and loquacious words are not spoken. Material efforts are directed towards further pursuit of the light and its revelation. A man and a man are naught but a man; but a man illuminated is as a god, but not God. The lower is a man of law; the higher is a man of truth. One must perish, the other may live abundantly. There is no purpose higher than truth, which is not found in books nor in letters, but in the Word which is Light, and the Light which is in Silence. Know then, that the chain of ignorance shall not hold every man forever, because it is through temporal death that mankind is relaxed from its burden of suffering. Only when they have become weary of the ceaseless cycle will they choose to open their eyes and remove the veil.

14. This does not threaten the laws of man, except that the enlightened have no need of them. The laws do not bring aid; they command, and do not heal; they are manifest in society, but do not take away mankind's feebleness: but it does prepare the way for the mind, by providing a directive. This is similar to a child who must first be guided to right measure before

discovering that the measure is a map of the road, but not the road itself. Mankind was threatened by its own self defeating adversity; he did not wish to awaken, and for fear that he should become awakened, he boasted that he already was so. The law was created to ensure the comfort of his illusion, and it bound him; he finds himself accused, now, he exclaims against the bondage. Is there no pleasing mankind? No. For the only departure from man's self imposed conflict is to become other than human, more than human, illuminated by truth. The seeking of gnosis is not without its dangers, nor its sufferings. As the initiate has chosen to remove himself from the cycle, the body and the mind rebel. As the body becomes illumined by the light, the material reality will take on a subtle seduction, attempting to dissuade the pursuant. As the initiate pursues the light of gnosis, certain forces will attempt to control the initiate, through both obvious manipulation and subtle suggestion. As the Light replaces the darkness, the animal may become enamored with the glamour and fall short. Let not your eye be deceived, let not your fears be realized, and do not step from the path, for the true path to Light is as narrow as a razor's edge.

15. I speak, my brethren, regarding the silence of the initiate who walks in the Light. Who can speak regarding the majesty of illumination, and the divinity within each being? In explaining and speaking of illumination, to do so in any fashion we find ourselves not sufficient, indeed wholly insufficient: we do not endeavor to fill up to your thoughts with weighty opinion and uninformed rumor. Consider the silence in and of itself. But who may explain it to us, unless we declare it? Let the Word declare itself within. Better does the mind declare itself within, than one who speaks without. Let the Light itself show to you the grace of gnosis, which has begun to dwell in your hearts. But now, if in explaining and setting forth its practice we are deficient, who can speak of divine revelation? If the Word disturbs us, who shall explain "In the beginning was the Word"? Keep hold then, brethren, of the silence whose language has no words, whose

senses are not comprehended by the lower mind of man, but only by the higher mind of the illumined. You will know you have arrived when the glow of the Light manifests around your body and your mind. You will know you are practicing correctly when body and mind become perfected in a state of torpor and illusion dies.

16. Through a servant was the law given, and made men guilty: by a saint was pardon received, and delivered the guilty into a realm of different measure. The servant is only able to act according to the law, but cannot release from the guilt of the law.

17. Perhaps anyone could say, "No one has seen God at any time." Then how is God to become known to humanity? For no one can know Truth except through silence, and how common is that? The secret of silence is found in the sitting, not in the lying down. It is in the yoking of the thoughts, which are too often wasteful and anemic. It is in the breath, which is the life. It is in the discipline through which one lives, and the maintenance of a clear perception, free of judgment and fear. There is no Judgment necessary when Truth is the lens through which the universe is viewed. There is no Fear when Death is no longer absolute. I do not come to you and ask you for empty faith and offer false hope, these are the signs of the demonic. I only offer you guidance to the truth which dispels all falsehood. There are no sages among the world's religions that can discern the true shape of God. They cannot present God to the common man. Occasionally, they can play parlor games to trick the mind, such as are used by Moses and the Egyptian Priests. They hide behind the mask of sacred virtue and popular fictions. It is true, God is fathomless, but not unknowable. The Christ is known to have said "the Kingdom of Heaven is within you and all around you." I tell you simply that the kingdom of heaven is the choice to create your own synchronicity, to make your own future as positive as possible. Fear and judgment destroy positivity, and project the Kingdom farther into the unknowable.

18. But know this, that all those things of the material world are not the sustenance of man. When we say silence, we do not merely mean silence of one's tongue, but the silence of one's mind through concentration and the cultivation of meaningful thoughts. The body is not the person, it is only a vehicle for thought, an interface used to move through the world. Irrational thoughts lead to misuse of the vehicle. Is it not said, "Blessed are the pure of heart, for they shall see God"? Like attracts Like, and so one's thoughts, the symbol and reflection of the external world, will ultimately attract similar circumstances to what is dwelt upon. "The Kingdom of Heaven is in you and all around you." Whatever is made manifest in the universe is done so through the body. What is seen is done so through the lens of the eye and the filter of one's pretext — there are none among you who are unbiased. But the removal of judgment is necessary for growth and enlightenment. How is this possible? Judgment is not sensory thought. Judgment is the ability to reconcile between one thing and another, but to the eye there is no difference — all is light. And even so, the light itself is merely detected by the eye, and is not processed. This process is done by the mind, which discerns what we see and when we see it. Is it not so with the eye of the mind, that when you are seeking your keys, they are on the table where you left them? In spite of the times you've looked over the table, they were not seen, they were not there. Have you hallucinated their absence? Just so, positive hallucination is as real as any other reality, to the body and to the mind. It may also be shared between people, and one will affect the other miraculously. The vision of Mary to the Catholics will heal and make fertile. The Fountain of Lourdes will heal the flesh and manifest great change in the patient. Ayurvedic medicine will heal the person of its greatest affliction — itself. For those visible and bodily appearances took place though the creature, in which a type might be exhibited: not in any fashion was the substance itself shown and made manifest. Give heed, beloved brethren, to this easy proof. Think upon as many things as are true, as many as are

righteous, as many as are pure, as many as are lovely, as many as are of good report, if any worthiness, and if any praise, think upon these things.

19. On this process, observe the purity of the body too, for its passage also affects the mind. God experiences the world through the experience of mankind, as we are the vehicle and co-creator of the universe with God. Just so must we make for our bodies to be a fitting Temple for God. One's psychology affects the behaviors, and consequently, ones behaviors affects the body. Addiction is known to harm the body because of the influence of the mind. Observe the behavior, and neutralize its addictions. Observe the mind, its processes, and how it is affected by these changes. It is not the drug which creates the addiction, but the mind. Cure the mind, and the drug goes on its own. Just so with behaviors as are found in the mentally ill. "Whosoever commits sin is the servant of sin." Not in some satanic manner, but in life's reflective nature. The overuse of any substance is dangerous to the body, it kills it in a subtle manner over many years. No human dies of "natural" causes, nor of "old age", but through the poisons consumed over a lifetime. Because we are not able to comprehend the invisible, we are held by the rules of the visible. Do not believe that the invisible ceases to affect us, as radiation, magnetism, and vibration affect us as surely as any knife. Every man is born dead, it is only the time through which we live and breath that we can change our behaviors positively, effectively, and permanently from life to life. Man is created whole, and even those dysfunctions inherent in the species may be overcome through the power of thought, of Light, and of the Word, which is infinite Silence. Can you change your reflection? Indeed, with practice, anything is possible. How soon forgetful are we, the mind affected by time, shocked into slavery of the animal desires, and defeated through submission by heavy handed law. There is no law of man which cannot be broken, and so they are impure and unreal. They are not laws, but rules, and rules have a way of affecting the mind in a contrary manner. Laws are unchanging and permanent, just as silence is. It exists even

amidst noise, a blank canvas upon which noise is painted. St. Lucifer is not here to present you with laws, for Love is the Law. Above this, there is no other.

20. What use is an eternal life to a mind that is forgetful? What use is the perfection of self and the attainment of enlightenment if we are not to enjoy it? To find the truth in silence is a simple task, but virtually impossible for most humans to practice. So simple does inaction seem, for most people perform in this way unconsciously, heeding only their own random thoughts, or the thoughts and beliefs of others. None of this is real. As the mind is commanded, so will it function. A mind guarded from manipulation, whose silence is practiced in a powerful and effective manner, who cultivates light in the mind, and consciously moves through the world in a body emptied of poisons and free of addiction, is one which will live longer, experience the condition of light, and be made ready for thought to function in a radically different manner. The practice is its own reward. The beauty of this world will be made available to the meek, but not to the weak of mind.

Invocation

To Rule over the Inferior, I call upon the celestial souls and the father of their manifold power. That every one of these souls is said to have double virtue, in knowing, and in governing its body. There are more deities in the heavens both above and below than there have been souls on earth. But there is only one Divine countenance whose might transcends the importance of every celestial body. Whose number is naught in one, one in naught. In glory do we call upon you to light the way to divine illumination. You, who contains the light of the stars, the Prince of the World, by whose light and splendor gives life to all things: Darkening, burning, overcoming virtue by your approach. The first mind, the mind which is life, the mind which is light, whose love transcends all bounds. You, who in the beginning made all things to join in diversity of sexes together in divine love: You who in great rejoicing called in the universe by many names, overcoming all things by your power. Humble the high to the low, the strong to the weak, the noble to the vile, and make clear the equality of all things, for in you every number is equal, there is no difference. Oh Divine Illumination, who brings light to all obscurity, opening the doors to the most secret mysteries. Oh Enlightenment, arbitrator of the Celestials, eloquent interpreter between the supernal and the infernal, open my eyes to that which is dark. Oh Beautiful Light, you have taught the secrets of the ways to divine nature. It is through your presence here that I educate my mind to the secrets within the glorified temple. Holy art Thou, the Mind of All. Holy art Thou, the Will become Law. Holy art Thou, giver of divine illumination. Holy art Thou, Power beyond knowing. Holy art Thou, worth beyond measure. Holy art Thou, above all praises. Accept this sacrifice from a pure soul and a yearning heart. You who are Nameless! You who are Formless! I praise you with Silence. Shed down upon me the Light of Illumination; show down your Light to the dark corners of the Earth. I will walk with you into the fires of an ignited mind. Whose number is naught in one, one in naught.

In you, whose nursing hands have brought me to light. Behold, the Beautiful One has come with wings of light, swirled round by the winds of heaven! Glowing black, radiant blindness, you have ushered me through the Valley in the shadow of death, you have guided and protected me, where many before me have remained unborn. You who now guides me still, from the darkness of ignorance into the light of everlasting illumination!

I am the uncreated god. Before me the dwellers in chaos are naught but shadows. I gather the power from every place, from every person, faster than light itself. Hail to thee above the heavens, thou who art stronger than even the terror of the darkness. Oh Holier than Holy, who gathers the power from every place, from every person, faster than light itself. Restore the giver of life. Create the gods from silence and comforts them. Bestow upon me this power from every place, from every person, faster than the shadow follows the light. Praise unto Thee, master of eternity, bringer of the everlasting, whose forms are manifold, whose works are mighty. Praise to Thee, who created the gods in your own image, who raised up the sky, who spread out the ground; who made those below and those above. Open the doors of heaven, throw open the sky to me. The womb of Night is filled with the seed of Life which is in her. The earth bends beneath our feet. Rise and rejoice, carry me with you, Immortal and Unending. Beneath me the Earth, Above me the Air, Before me the Fire, Behind me the Water. The doors of heaven are open, the doors of the Sky are open to me. Praise Thou, Oh body of Truth, whose shrine is hidden from the vulgar eyes of mankind, and from whose mouth the Vibration of the Universe came into being. As high as is the heaven, as broad as is the earth, as deep as is the sea, as brilliant as the sun. Above me stretches the Creature of Heaven. Beneath me lies the Lord of the Earth. Before me rises the beloved Children of the Hidden Light. Behind me shine the Holy names even the gods themselves do not speak "Bism Allah, Tawakalto A'la Allah" All delight in You, O Golden Light!

Mysterious Light who gives birth to Divinity; The Mind which forms the Model; Luminous One who thrusts back the darkness, who illuminates every living soul with its rays, Great One of many Names. Thou, who causes the Living Breathe; O Venerable Mother; Thou, who Rules the beatings of the Heart. It is the Golden One...the Creature of Darkness who illuminates the Soul from within. The Universe is filled with Joy, the Earth is full of gladness, the Heavens rejoice! Come, O Golden Illumination, for thou art the nourishment of the heart, the shining of the Inner Light. Nothing more is desired. I praise thee, Golden Majesty, Master of Heaven; Ruler in the Sanctuary; The One Shining as Gold in the Sanctuary of the Sun. I praise Your Manifestation to the Limitlessness of your Rays. Powerful One, Oh Great One! Dweller upon the Horizon, Holiness of Heaven, Brilliant One who creates the rays of the Sun; The Beautiful, with numerous colors, The Only One in the sky, May I go in and out, pure of hands, pure of Soul. Thou who art called the Unique One, Terror among the Guardians of the Earth who bow their heads at your passing. You illuminate the World with the Rays of Your Eye. The South, the North, the West, and the East pay you homage, and they make adoration to your beauty. The Great Sovereign of Heaven, The Beautiful Light, the One who gives sight to the blind, Who is called the Lesser, but is Greater in the Eyes of Man! The August and Powerful One; Oh Thou the Perfection of Self! I adore Your Majesty with Your heart's desire. I invoke Your Image with the sacred texts, Come in peace, progress in joy; my heart is sweetened by your presence. Words spoken by the Great God, Master of Heaven: Adoration as you rise, by the praises of the Foremost of the Universe, in the midst of the justified, justified before All. Every pure and good thing, every sweet and enduring thing belongs to Thee. Powers of the Storm, Fires of Heaven, Wheel within the Wheel. Thou art the Angel of the Chariot that goes in every direction at once; Full of eyes, all seeing. You have given me the Kabbalah of the Soul, and have Revealed the Work by which the soul can reach the ever higher dimensions of consciousness. You have related the paths the soul may travel toward ultimate realization. Unite the Finite with the Infinite in the perfection of divine personality. Provide a new illumination of human possibilities. Grant the soul self-realization: love, power, knowledge, holiness, and unification. The four-faced Chayot: the bull-ox, lion, eagle, and man bow to Thee. Envision within Yourself Mankind on the throne to become His divine higher self, the knowledge that defines the secret doctrine of the whole of the mystical tradition culminated in the Holy Kabbalah. Arise in the Horizon of Heaven, In the Boat of Millions of Years. You are the Great Defender! Great one of magic, eternal is your name, illuminator of night, you who soothes the sleepless and disheveled spirit, the Vault of Heaven. The Unborn Seed of Night grows with Illuminate intentions, and its radiance glows in the full face of my actions. Oh, Endless Night, Keeper of the Keys to the Vault of Heaven, your name on my tongue and on my lips, the milk of your breast feeds me, the glimmer of uncountable stars glows through me. Deny me arrogance, and fill me with gnosis, the truths overlooked by nations.

Compromiser gladly compromised, Seducer gladly seduced: Know my Love everlasting. Guard of the doors of perception, grant me the key of true vision, the light above and the light below; in the darkness and in the light you are hidden, open now for me. The vision rises, unfolding the contours of a thousand hidden faces amidst the foliage of earth, the leaves of red fire, the spun petals of woven water, and the sweet winds of the sky kiss my face. Gracious keeper, open the portal to my thoughts, that the secrets within will become my secrets, in silence and in truth everlasting.

Unspeakable, unmistakable, and uncomprehending did you move upon the face of the waters, separating land from sea, fire from air. I gaze upon the rapturous face and see within it an unconquerable muse: rouse the spirits that keep sanction to the inner gates of the mind. You, who are a part of my perfected being, rise within me, act through me, bring me closer to your womb, that I may be reborn on the moment of this utterance.

We therefore come together, all minds in one, one mind in the multitude. I ask of We, Mind of my Mind, in Silence and in secret, saying, "Will you at this time restore again the kingdom?" And Mind of my Mind said to me, "You are witness to the Mind of Mind, this is the kingdom of which you seek, the Malkuth in Kether, the Kether in Malkuth. There is no other." Then I saw a new heaven and a new earth, for the first heaven and the first earth had passed away for me, and there was no longer any sea, or sky, or fire, or earth.

"Now the dwelling of God is within mankind, and the Light will live within them. They are a people without need of Law, and the Light itself will be with them and live through them. There will be no more death or mourning or crying or pain, for the order of such profane existence has no meaning. There is only the truth which exists from life to life.

In Lux, In Vita, In Amare, In Nomine Lucina Dea. Amen. In nomine, Spiritus Sancti, Amen.

Review of Spiritual Science

It is our tenet that God by any other name is still God, which is "Undifferentiated Be-ing", and which is wholly unconcerned with an individual's or assemblage's dogmatic opinion based on the principle that God is so much more than can be conceived of by the imagination of mankind. In this all religions are equalized. In this, all religions are collections of human inaccuracy.

I find it interesting that a human being can go through life without ever having been aware. There is an infinite universe of wisdom hidden within the world you perceive everyday, and slowly humanity is awakening from the slumber of materialism, the unfolding of mankind's inner evolution. There is a sealed door in most people's minds which may remain invisible and unstirred for entire lifetimes. When these doors of perception eventually open, "Life" becomes transformed from a purposeless darkness of obscurity to a universe of purposeful illumination.

Unlike the teachings of common religious philosophy, which teach that the universe is the creation of a God who is unknowable, untouchable, and unapproachable, true Wisdom is found within our own Key to Awareness of what the universe is. Perception once thought of as simply an illusion of opinion and pseudo-philosophy, now becomes the canvas of our personal reality. With it we may shape an entire universe with instruments of the imagination, the mind, and the power of a belief built - not out of faith - but out of practical conviction in a science for those who would first master themselves.

It seems inevitable that something different must come from the turbulent times we live in: either a higher frequency of enlightenment or annihilation. The swing of the pendulum is the wave upon which we experience this evolution; through our reactions we are able to counteract all of the cruelty and brutality. Kindness must beget kindness in the psychology of mankind.

This is, in fact, one of the greatest gifts of the saints, and the premise of the Pavlovian lesson. Science has shown us that the mind, when given the choice between a negative and a positive outcome, will choose positive or neutral. Every behavior is implemented by the mind to fulfill a condition, and every action is justified through unconscious conditioning or conscious programming.

If negativity did not so quickly burn itself out, humanity would have destroyed itself long ago. We must disagree with the harbingers of doom, cynics and misanthropes who believe that to be "human" must mean that we must inevitably fail. These are the people who witness the lethargy of the common person who has not been taught any behavior other than "limitation" and "conformity". In fact, this very sense of incompetence and ineptitude is so common that we have at our disposal a supply of ready and willing slaves to our cause — whatever cause it happens to be. It has been said by wiser men than myself that, if one is not willing to take action for them-selves, they will certainly be put to use for the fulfillment of someone else's goal. Indeed, the successful adept is not the same as the common person who is under-confident and overly-comfortable in a world of worry, suffering, and stress.

Yet, due to some unseen momentum, mankind continues to move towards enlightenment. We suffer every form of distraction from this most superior goal: luxury, poverty, ignorance, intellectualism, oppression, profiteering, blind fanaticism, antipathy, prejudice, emotionalism, and all other forms of psychological deviation. But even so, barriers of race, religion and class are slowly being dissolved. We are beginning to discover the myriad forms of tyranny and oppression. We are waking up from stagnation, and the opiate called materialism. We strive blindly for comfort, for "peace of mind", and for amusement — all the while finding comfort in chaos, "peace of mind" in unhappiness, and amusement in cruelty.

Such contradictions exist within us. But wait, behind this is a secret, an evolution moving through the throes of adolescent angst and obscenity. We are moving through this age into another. I am not so crass to consider that the "Age of Aquarius" is the age of wisdom, but I do see in the analogy some truth.

Struggling to mature within us is another analogy - one of alchemical transition, from a long Dark Age to a new awakening of the Age of Spirit, where our material fermentation ignites in the spirit of man, through a psychological Calcination we burn off everything except the pure gold within...the Perfected Self. What this means on an individual level is the destruction of our "ego", our attachments and become purified through self-evaluation and introspection. Indeed the genius' amongst us, - the Adepts of our race - the magicians and mystics who have moved beyond their own personal agendas and into a state of ecstasy have used this very method.

In this ecstatic universe of perception underlying every thought, every word, every action, hides the siddhas — magical powers that lay dormant in the common human being. It is not until a complete awakening and the development of control over oneself that these siddhas become fully active, that the transcendence of common humanity occurs.

Every religion, from the simple shamanistic religions to the most ritualized and canonized mystery traditions believe in magical powers of some sort. Superstition and Taboo are cultural traditions and a reality in the world, even today in this "modern" Dark Age. As C. G. Jung made so perfectly clear to those who would listen with an objective ear, the mythologies in our religions and stories follow the same general pattern in the mind — an Archetype system of correspondence similar to the Occult (non-Hebrew) Kabbalah.

If we were to survey the history of mankind's intellectual development, certain geniuses will stand out. These giants among men taught the laws, the sciences, and the mysteries of the universe. They have done more in preparation for the technologies that you now enjoy than has actually been accomplished in this "Industrial" era. What they practiced looked deep into the structure of reality, what many of us do today is to merely accept what is given us at face value. Ignorance and Ineptitude. We exist upon thousands of years of scholarship and all of the explanations of the sages and philosophers who precede us.

Pythagoras said "God Geometrizes." He understood that the universe is structured on a system of exact mathematical vibrations, harmonies, dimensions, frequencies, &c. All of these have exact patterns in mathematics and geometry. Behind these teachings are the hidden forces of the universe that may be tapped through the same disciplines and methods of study that the intellectual giants preceding us followed. These people turned their minds away from petty personal issues to concentrate on this very study, the higher understanding of the universe in all of its subtlety. Those who understand how a universe works may also use that understanding to direct that universe in much the same manner as one would any tool.

The human brain contains five times as many physical brain cells as the average person brings to use. Besides understanding the material universe it also has access to the finer strata of the astral universe, those subtle places of the soul. The brain is much like a wireless receiver. With the right practices the magician can learn to tune in to any frequency in the range of vibrations. The brain is the perfect instrument for the use of the Will and the Mind, but it is little understood, even by the science that claims that these abilities do not exist because they can't be empirically tested. This does not logically negate their reality, but instead shows the limitations of the scientific processes used. Until relatively recently many forms of vibration were unheard of, such as x-rays and radio frequencies. Because mysticism requires such dedicated practice, persistence of study and the determination to see the entire science through to its completion, very few people are able to practice it to its fullest potential. Even the common person finds simple meditation incredibly difficult, even though those who have practiced it show remarkable results after a relatively short period of consistent practice. There are latent abilities hidden in every person, but it is commonly neither understood nor used.

It is understood by those who have begun to awaken from that dreadful sleep of ignorance that most people are only "Awake", that is "completely and consciously aware of the present moment", for a maximum of 5 minutes each day. The rest of the day is spent in redundant and repetitive programming — conditioned responses and wasted thoughts (worry, frustration, reaction, conditioned responses, &c.). In fact, most people have accepted this illusion as their reality, and do not realize that it is no more "real" than the pages in a fantasy novel. It is a surprise to we who know that with only an average of 5 minutes of wakefulness we have, as a species, been able to accomplish so much! Imagine, if we were awake for the entirety of our day, what are we capable of?

Each human being has the potential to accomplish miracles, to perform feats of greatness, to develop within themselves perfect genius and wisdom, and to access unlimited creativity. In fact, each and every person is as powerful as they allow themselves to be. But this potential is so often smothered and kept out of reach by vast layers of inhibitions, redundant thought patterns, habitual behaviors, fears, worries, laziness as well as other such debilitating, stagnant and static thought forms.

Mankind must take the largest possible view of the universe, instead, as of now, the most restricted. According to the size of one's mental horizon so will be size of one's perceptions, and thus one's power be. A person's limitations are of their own making, and have no reality except that belief gives them. "Nothing is either good or bad, but thinking makes it so." – Hamlet

Merely as an experiment, this is worth trying, regardless of one's belief system, religion, dogma, philosophy or representations of the universe. It is impossible to contemplate the actuality of these methods without taking active part in them. One may presuppose that these methods are real, and one may even choose to believe in them blindly, but one cannot gain even a modicum of true and stable belief without experience. Intellectualizing about a concept will only take one so far without any real activity. Those who are content to regurgitate the memorized, plagiarized and often misquoted material without actively practicing for themselves are the worst kind of redundant, effete, and pretentious pseudo-philosophers there are.

It is said by the scientists that "...metaphysical theories can't be empirically tested..." (- R.T. Carroll). This is the worst kind of ignorance. Because the instrumentation has not yet been created to measure a certain kind of energy does not mean that this energy does not exist. As much as is known about the universe by mankind would not even amount to a grain of sand amongst all grains upon the beach. Even in magnetic field research new information is discovered every day. Much of science exists as theory, and theory without practice will ever remain theory. Metaphysics is known in many schools of practical mysticism. Many of the siddhas, or magical powers, are the signs to success and the assurance that one is indeed making progress. Unfortunately, the scientific community is unable to perceive that these skills are evidence of magical attainment, as so very few people practice magic along appropriate methodologies. Magicians with the ability to levitate on command are rarer still, among the adepts who remain hidden from the world, leaving the scientific communities search for statistical "proof" in perpetual darkness.

Scientific studies have been carried out with Yogis in India , who have shown great abilities that boggle the mind of the common Westerner. Government sponsored scientific research such as Remote Viewing has been developed with the understanding that psychic ability is a real and measurable effect.

Skeptic Organizations such as the James Randi Educational Foundation take it as "reality" that such abilities do not exist, based on the fact that no one has ever passed their tests. Psychics are accused of "Cold Reading " or "manipulating", regardless of their accuracy. Most people who have developed the ability to read tarot know that the use of analogy and metaphor in a reading is the very heart of psychic readings. A psychic is not merely a clairvoyant as so many might assume. The psychic is able to determine while in a state of trance the lines of correlation between one abstract symbol and another, while relating the meaning to the client. Skeptics do not consider "percentage" of accuracy as any indication of psychic ability. They must "Prove" with an accuracy of 100%, within absolute protocols. As has been written elsewhere, psychology is the least empirical of sciences, and all forms of self perfection must first begin with a change in perception of what is possible and what can occur, even on the outside chances of probability. Determining what is likely is not the same as gauging what is possible. Scientific statistics will not gauge "Laziness", and would only hypothesize that some brain chemistry is at fault. Though brain chemistry may be affected through ones behavior, it is not the reason why behaviors become repetitive. This is called "Associative Conditioning", proven by Pavlov and put to use through modern psychology.

Following this change in perception is the changing in behavior through introspection and self evaluation. This requires the ability to perceive a model of what the person wishes to become —

a self-created role model. In history this has been any sort of Hero, Deity, God, &c. We have a tendency to desire what belongs to others, and thus give up our True Will for the illusion of satisfaction. In fact, we identify ourselves through our associations with those things in our environment. To avoid this pitfall, the magician has devised a spiritual role model called the "Perfected Self". This is similar to the "Higher Self" or the "Holy Guardian Angel". The Perfected Self is yourself in the distant (or not so distant) future, the perfect and enlightened "you" that is in the process of becoming. This is ultimately the goal of every soul, to attain this level of illumination. This is the highest Order that humanity can attain to and still remain human. It is the complete realization of the Divinity within. Many people have called this the "Conversation with the Holy Guardian Angel", but "Conversion with the Perfected Self" would describe our method much more effectively.

Because this Perfected Self is perfectly Illumined, it is beyond all temptation, beyond all Ego, and beyond all forms of obscurity that mankind is heir to. This BE-ing is beyond space and time, beyond limitation. It is as perfect as God, but still only a child of God, not yet itself a God, lacking still the ability to maintain a macrocosm outside of itself. It has moved beyond all desire and into a perception of pure Holiness.

The Invocation of this Perfected Self is much more desirable than the Invocation of God, as God is so much more than we as limited creatures can imagine. Every "vision" of God has its limitations in the imagination faculties of man. We are presently imperfect, and thus have not the capability to comprehend God in IT's limitlessness. "There are more things in heaven and earth, Horatio, than are dreamt of in your philosophy." (Ibid.) God is pure, undifferentiated Be-ing, and cannot be accurately described as anything else. (In this is the secret of all cosmologies and dogmas proven false. Every "Law" of God is a law of man, having no relation to God's Will except through Religion (discipline, restraint, institutionalized conformity).

The invocation of this Perfected Self draws us towards it, creating within us a union of divine force with our conscious reality. We move from Unconscious Incompetence (that is, inability to perceive the Divinity within ourselves, ignorance), to Conscious Incompetence (the ability to recognize our imperfection, and yearn towards that divine state), to Conscious Competence (the utilization of the Methods of Invocation to bring one towards Illumination), and finally to Unconscious Competence (where we have attained the Siddhas and have begun conversion with our Perfected Selves to the point where we are becoming so much more than what is commonly accepted as "Human", where our aspiration to Realizing our own Divinity takes form in our behaviors and Illumination).

This Perfected self cannot be tainted by our Invocation, as it has itself moved beyond limitation. We in turn purify and initiate ourselves through consistent and repetitive practice of the invocation. This is where "Touch and be touched" no longer applies to the magician who has moved outside of the common destiny of mankind. We are no longer, thus, ruled by the stars, no longer subject to another person's Will, no longer controlled by our habitual and conditioned behaviors. We become fully aware every moment, exhibiting the attainment of perfect Dharma and Presence. This attainment and the fulfillment of one's Role as an Illuminated Be-ing is the True Will spoken of by so many, who themselves little understood the concept.

What is it that the members of the Illuminati (Children of the Light) wish to accomplish with these abilities? The Obligation of every member of the Order is to "...the Preservation and Stewardship of the Global Environment, the Enlightenment of the Race of Mankind, and the Perfection of Self." This is accomplished through a particular curriculum of magical practice.

The methods of the Order are specific to our needs: there is not a word wasted, neither is there an action performed that is not designed to accomplish a specific goal or purpose. All material trappings have been avoided where possible, as the magician need not be robed in dogmatic regalia to reveal insignia of empty stations of attainment. No trappings of the occult world are utilized except in the grace of ritual. Tradition is maintained where useful, discarded where unnecessary.

The Novice preparation is no less an honor to the Initiate. It is the degree of learning, the practice to perfection, and expands the abilities of the mind and the soul so that it can experience and accomplish things which would have been incomprehensible and uncongenial to it before. Within the Novice Grade exist all of the previously discovered stages of development, though the Vault may be given to members who have shown a particular aptitude for the method and manner of the siddhas.

Meanwhile, most of humanity is ignorant of the existence of such a universe where magical attainment is possible. They are tired and depressed, bewildered by black and white rules in a world that seems inextricably mixed, poisoned and stupefied by wrong living and habitual behaviors of every kind. Humanity has neither the intellect nor the time for study and research, nor for self-analysis and introspection. Humanity is therefore in danger of missing the joy and wonder of enlightenment and the reawakening to a life of opportunity which such a life brings. The siddhas and wisdom teachings must again become comprehensible to each and every one of us once more.

Philosophy of Silence

It is the method of our philosophy to attract only the most advanced practitioners, the most dedicated to the cause of perfecting their own minds. It is the seeking of divine illumination, which attracts, like all substances, its own kind. The stronger the light, the stronger the attraction. There is a magnetic pull among like minds that can be seen amongst the secular humans in a very broad manner, that is more of a psychological manifestation than a magical one. The premise is the same for the occult, that like attracts like, and that the most adept will attract other adepts of a similar caliber and grade.

Just so, there are very many people attracted to the practices, which are occult or metaphysical in nature. These range between the vaguely interested who swallow whole any impression offered - no matter how unrealistic, to the insatiable appetites who desire power over the material universe on a spiritual dimension, because they cannot do so on the physical. We are not, and cannot illuminate the former, and avoid with just pretension the latter, for they have often proven themselves to be among the worlds most eloquent and garrulous of our kind. These provide a brilliant cover for the practices of the true adept, who does not share their practices with another, for true spirituality never advertises itself.

Our kind has no paraphernalia, no obvious religion, and do not share our practice except with those with whom we practice with. It is our nature to study with perseverance the nature of our minds in both the manner of psychology, and of the outer fringes of the human mind itself, the powers of consequence. These are the rare occurrences of the manipulation of occult abilities, which evade normal human scientific evaluation. It is not the absence of evidence which proves that the material is the only universe, for science has discovered many "invisible" items such as ionizing radiation, electromagnetic fields, radio frequencies, to name a few of the more representative discoveries. These lead to the innovations which every person may make use of, much as the telephone and MRI, stereo and computer. These too came from a previously undiscovered material called "electricity", which every child understands today. But the sciences of the mind are barely understood at all, and are quashed as entirely unimportant to the common person, and in many cases, entirely hidden in the occult universe of Government Agencies who would exploit them for covert manipulation (and justly so, for information is power, and the power is maintained by those who have the ability to use it. The government is not as ignorant as the common person would imagine.)

In this manner then, are the true occultists kept hidden from the world by a multi-layered veil, in the seclusion of temporal obscurity. The occultist does not speak out publicly, keeping the true power away from those who would abuse it, and who could not possibly use it appropriately. Proof of this is everywhere, and is the cause of this paper: spells for money, periapts for love, invocations for power, Svengali hypnosis, television subliminals, and covert manipulation disguised as music. This series of veils is what makes the true occult both prized and of permanent demand. The common uninitiated public cannot hope to delve into the mysteries, because access requires the keys of the mind, and these keys are immediately recognizable at the gates – none may enter without the secrets fully understood. One will not find these in books, nor recorded in any manner available to the public. It is of a paradoxical nature, and cannot be explained in simple gestures and subtle signs. It is not a secret, which is passed around in the manuscripts of sigils and instruction. It is not a passive event sought by the outer mind. It is not found in ritual and dogma, nor in theory and practice. It is not in the commonly supposed creative symbolism that the power of the soul is to be sought, but instead is found in the silence and non-movement of the mind.

The silence is a secret, for it only grants the secrets of the mind to its own – the people who seek will not find, but those who wish in earnest to develop themselves to perfection will be given entrance. With Love, Light and Life, will find the solace they seek, and will not leave empty handed. This is the bitter root of the common uninitiated occultist, for as available as the rituals and symbolism of the ancients are made available by the scholarly, they will do little good to the initiate who is not initiated to silence. Just so, the most commonly accepted magical powers are those that are subtle, for it is only through coincidence that they have any success. The great powers of old are fallen victim to literature and Deus ex Machina; not so for those who would not speak. The paranormal is no longer simply hallucination or manipulation of the numbers, it is not simply a quaint spell whispered or shouted to the stars as a supplication to powers that are already extinguished, for the initiated are subject to the powers which are unavailable to the common seeker. The Gods will not answer to the profane. Coincidence and psychological factors aside, the secret is only found in silence, for the silence itself is the secret guardian of the gates of the mind. In meditation is the true initiation found, not in hallucination and guided pathworking. These are fit to the uninitiated occultist, who would fill her time with practices intended to fill her time, but in the seeking will not find the power she so desperately searches for. (One often-frustrated seeker stumbled upon the key, "If invoked without lust for results, it is the single most powerful force that an individual can possess.")

The initiate often asks that, if it so simple, why do we have so many texts regarding the occult, the paranormal, the new age, metaphysics, and other such manuals of symbol and ritual? Mankind is filled with admiration for itself, and addicted to its own magnificence. We are not concerned with knowledge, but with pattern. Science is developed to test theories regarding pattern within behavior, both human and natural, so that others may reproduce results of their manipulation with exponential success. Learning in today's society is an imposed endeavor, forced on children from a young age to teach discipline and basic life skills; individuals rarely learn to educate themselves by their own volition. Where a child is given the basic needs by rote, our society creates a chasm for the mind, so that any information repeated with effort becomes "knowledge", or a thing known, but not necessarily understood. Metaphysical books are a dime a dozen, and less so if we account for the lack of accurate data. Occult books are somewhat more expensive, but teach the metaphorical, not the truly occult, for this can only be found within, and is rarely expressed in a vocal manner, and never to the uninitiated. Theory and Ritual are fantastic concepts to keep the mind busy, where the true occultist seeks to still the mind, and seeks language without words — it is obvious when this is realized that the illustrations and specialized vocabulary are shared and studied, while the true occultists have moved through the ever-growing mountain of "knowledge" and instead seeks true gnosis. Those unprepared minds will find only silence, the truly prepared will find the truth in the silence.

Similarly, the occultists have resolved the crisis of charlatanry by drawing the curtain on its practices, and the silence itself is the key to occultism's secret. The works of the common teach patterns which may be created in language, and similarly, any information which is accidentally stumbled upon in the darkness of the mind is accepted by the population en masse. But the secrets of the ancients will remain hidden to the imperfect and the unresolved until such a time as they truly seek perfection. Until then, only those rare individuals who seek after the Light itself will find it, and to darkness with the rest.

Machine Psychology

It is not my intention to discuss the Theory of Reality, but that reality itself is a theory.

Science

The science of modern man has created rules based on material reality and the "Double Blind" method of experimentation. This rule creates a bias towards human interaction with the data, without considering one important fact: Ones description of a THING is implied by one's interaction with a THING. We may boil water a million times, to completely understand how water boils under different circumstances, with different devices of measurement, and different kinds of equipment, this will never bring us any closer to understanding it. If we were to limit our very experience of the universe to the implicit experience of H2O, it's scientifically determined attributes and chemical make up, we might be able to DESCRIBE the properties of water, but it will not allow us to understand water any better than we had before.

This is similar to the realization that the description of a THING is not the thing itself. Imagine mistaking the MAP for the TERRAIN. Try traveling along a map and see how far you get. Maps are used as a DESCRIPTION, a REPRESENTATION of a THING. That does not make it any more REAL than the THING itself. Likewise, our scientific descriptions, no matter how accurate and detailed it may be, will never be the same as the THING itself.

Direct experience of a phenomenon is not REAL either. The experience immediately becomes MEMORY, which is in turn affected by a number of inconsistencies and contradictions. Like an echo, the memory is distorted leaving holes in awareness and becoming little more than a SYMBOL. One's direct experience of reality is therefore a function of the IMAGINATION, and is similar to HALLUCINATION.

Each memory is an IMPRESSION of a moment upon the brain. This impression is vulnerable to the same EROSION as any other object in our experience of nature. All reality then, is a DISTORTION.

Ones experience of sensory data is immediately distorted by the MODEL that we CREATE to describe that data. It is a distorted recreation of the actual phenomena perceived. A scientist is only as accurate as his instruments, and these too are imprecise and approximate. One's meticulous explanations of the data perceived are only as accurate as the person receiving the explanation.

A scientist attempts to describe phenomena existent in reality using a FILTER called Mathematics. This mathematical model is a language used to describe phenomena in a manner which may be shared with other scientists. It ignores Quality over Quantity. One need not understand the Atomic Weight of H_2O in order to drink it. If "scientific evidence" proves, for example, that water boils at 100 degrees Celsius, plus or minus the variations of foreign matter, gravitation and instrumentation, that temperature is considered by the SCIENTIFIC MODEL to be accurate, regardless of its prejudice to inaccurate methods of measurement. OBJECTIVE models do not exist, except in THEORY. Science, then, is a THEORY based on SUBJECTIVE measurements said to represent a mathematical model.

This mathematical model is the only true language, as it is EMPIRACLE and only biased where the numbers do not balance. The only assumption is that the Data is as accurate as the Model used to INTERPRET it.

The Scientific Philosophy is dedicated especially to a tangible reality system, assuming that those things perceived in a similar manner by MOST PEOPLE ARE the most accurate by consensus. This is in itself a delusion, for each person's model of reality is wholly unlike any other person's. We base this delusion primarily on the common language used to describe a THING, and forget that this model is not the experience itself. The assumption that each MIND experiences the universe in exactly the same manner is a limiting distortion. We cannot assume, for example, that the word "white" in one person's vocabulary is exactly the same as in another person's, as each person has different experiences associated with the term. Perhaps one person is blind or cannot differentiate between shades of color. To say the word "Ocean" to a desert dweller is associated with "Gibberish". To describe the concept of "Ocean" to a desert dweller will never pass on the "Idea" of an incalculable expanse of water.

That many do not believe in another's facts does not affect those who have had such direct genuine experiences. That science is wholly unable to comprehend such things as miracles - due to its physicalistic bias and method - does nothing whatever to explain away the incidence of these observable facts.

Religion

The mind is completely IMAGINATION. All thoughts are created out of speculation, whether logical or irrational. The MEMORY itself is imperfect. All remembered experience is a constantly shifting hallucination. Similarly, hallucination is much more common than is usually realized. Such things as NEGATIVE HALLUCINATION are common daily occurrences. In fact, it is an important part of our psychological behavior, allowing us to focus our immediate attention on one thing at a time.

Indeed, we would be overwhelmed with sensory data if we were to open the floodgates of awareness. Our eyes are limited to a specific wavelength of light vibrations; our ears to a specific wavelength of sound vibrations; our body creates natural chemicals called endorphins and opoiods which limit the sensory data received from our nervous system. We naturally ignore redundant information. Positive Hallucination occurs commonly in the form of day dreams and visualizations.

"Our minds take in information from the environment, combine it with aspects of memory, shape it to satisfy certain needs, and produce a belief that may or may not have anything to do with reality" - James Alcock

We must always be suspicious of our own experience. We must never take it as the arbiter of truth. Believers and skeptics often construct their belief systems in similar ways. Each learns from their social environment, and each tends to stereotype the other. Often, people may reject science as elitist, irrelevant, or closed-minded. Conversely, many believe that mystical, magical, or miraculous beliefs are inaccurate and hallucinated. In many ways, both are right. Skeptics will often use psychological terms to condemn psychology. Psychology will use the same psychological terms to examine scientists.

Christians, for example, can only identify with the writing in their Holy books, and consider any form of speculation upon them as occult force. Indeed, it is often stated that a Christian cannot argue his religion without using the BIBLE as reference. It becomes a self identifying belief system, ignorant and ill-mannered. The same arguments used against other belief systems may also be effectively used against Christianity. Islam, and the Muslim nation, has also forgotten that their religion was originally intended to awaken the reader to an acceptance of both logic and mysticism. Instead it has become a fundamentalist congregation, unable to think for itself, limited by its own fear of retribution.

All belief systems, regardless of their original intention or present condition, are merely models we use to explain the phenomena in our world. The belief in GOD is usually held by people who have never experienced IT. They call this FAITH, which means "Belief without evidence". Others call it GULLIBILITY, which also means "Belief without evidence".

The mystic has experiences that would qualify as personal evidence. Mysticism is a behavioral science which rightly examines the structure of ones personal experience of reality. Included in this system are practices specifically tailored to manipulate and control hallucinations, to develop control over one's own action, and to perfect the behavior over time. Because of the nature of human weakness, it is rare that we find a master of such ability that they are capable of miracles such as walking on water, levitation, transmutation of one matter into another, telepathy, telekinesis, and bi-location.

Interestingly enough, if a master were to one day appear who allowed science to "prove" the abilities and their causes, these would no longer be considered "Mystical", but would instead be under the jurisdiction of "Science", such as Alchemy, Mathematics, and Pharmacology, which were at one time called "Mystical" and "Magical". One could suppose, then that science is a matter of "Belief with Evidence", or REPRODUCIBLE RESULTS.

"We have effectively committed ourselves to the voluntary ASSUMPTION that the material universe is real, despite the inadequate nature of our minds to verify that that happens to be infallibly true. At every stage, our theories will continue to be incomplete and therefore fallible, but if we can use the theory to engineer ourselves some desired outcome, then we need not be concerned by the fact that the theory is fallible and focus on the fact that it did, in fact, help us to mold the material universe in a particular way. Engineering is possible even if the underlying science is bad or incomplete. At the same time, better and better theories and sciences will help us accomplish more and more practical engineering as we reveal more accurate theories about the material universe." - Karun Philip, Zen and the Art of Funk Capitalism

A Belief System is a Model of one's reality, a theory which may or may not be accurate, but which allows us to operate within the bounds of our theoretical universe. These bounds are our self imposed LIMITATIONS, and represent the probability of events occurring in conformity with our Theory.

Belief System = Model = Theoretical Universe

The model is not reality except to the individual experiencing it. The belief system affects the reality experienced by changing the bounds of limitation in any and all actions.

Philosophy

Psychology studies the mechanics of human behavior and cognition. It is understood by magicians that one's psychology is what decisions a person makes previous to taking action. Behavior is Action. The internal communication a person has with him or herself is the PROGRAMMING that defines one's belief system. This is created through repetition, regardless of the truth. People often believe lies and half truths. People are often unable to test a truth for accuracy. All truths are by their very nature WORDS which contain in them basic ASSUMPTIONS. These assumptions become arbitrary under some conditions, becoming GENERALIZATIONS. If all truths are generalizations, all truths are untrue. But the mind uses these assumptions as the programming language, regardless of this little truth.

The Scientific Theory which excludes human interaction cannot be used to determine hypnosis or communication. Both of these rely on strategic thought and the ability to become a BIOFEEDBACK mechanism. Communication requires one or both participants (id est, speaker and audience) to consciously or unconsciously feedback information received and use this to develop RAPPORT. Where Skepticism suggests that science is theoretical fact, Magic suggests that mysticism is practical application. Engineering does not require science to prove reality, only to give rules to build upon in manipulating that reality. If reality exists exclusively in the mind, then the mind is the key to understanding and influencing it.

Science uses a device called "Psychosomatic Medicine" to explain away certain phenomena, such as complete remissions of cancer from the body. They do not find it interesting that they require three types of study groups: a "control" group, a "test" group, and a "placebo" group. Where science refuses to accept the psychosomatic cure, they also use it as a counterpoint against their theory.

"Trials will also follow the traditional format involving a double blind study with a placebo group. In other words, some randomly selected subjects will get a pill or capsule that looks like the supplement or medication but which has no effect while others will get the actual supplement or medication being studied. Subjects won't know what group they are in and the doctors doing the assessments of their condition won't know either. This information won't be revealed until the end of the study period when all the data has been collected and submitted. Placebo groups are necessary if researchers are investigating symptoms that can be affected by the subject's beliefs and perceptions." - Marsha L. Miller, Ph.D.

Magic

Mysticism develops in the practitioner a basic psychological program for successful behavior. It also trains the MIND of the mystic to comprehend the unreality of the MODEL we experience. The mystic also understands that the mind may be trained to manipulate the model in a wholly different manner than the common person may. Meditation trains the mind to control its inner dialogue, and the physical mechanism of the body. Eventually, one gains control over the spirit itself and the mystic realizes his or her true divinity. From this point, it is possible to manifest changes in the outer shared reality, such as telepathy, telekinesis, levitation, &c. Enlightenment, or the conversion with one's Perfected Self, is model of one's Divine Being.

Secret Doctrine

The Secret Doctrine suggests that the whole world, and the entire universe, both subjective and objective, is illusory, and that MIND is the sole reality. The object of our senses, our bodily vehicle, our mental cognitions, inferences, generalizations, and deductions are a common delusion. Matter, organic and inorganic, has no true form and no true existence. Color and sound, all things seen by the eyes, are merely wavelengths, vibrations, and these vibrations, although measurable, are transient and ever changing. Space, dimension, time, force, and matter are vibrations, energies, with only a ghost form created by our own minds to comprehend and manipulate what we perceive. Consciousness is our interface and our filter. It is in direct contact with the thought form of reality, and edits the information received through our belief system and eventually becomes perception. Nothing natural or supernatural can be proven to exist beyond this reality model that we create for ourselves. And each reality model is different from another.

"…the skeleton of Science was formed by the Philosophers. Mathematics was developed, and there was evolved the lasting method of investigating actual phenomena and writing down the results of experiments or observations such as involved matter, force, time and space - the Scientific Method. Scientific investigation was then, and still is, a process of mixing various combinations of the two elements, force and matter, within, the limitations of time and space, then carefully observing the results and drawing conclusions from them. Stars, chemical combinations in a laboratory, the metabolism of the body - all such things are the sum total of the materials of Science. Observing, measuring and fabricating new and useful combinations, these are the total activities of Science. There is nothing mysterious about Science or its methods which is deserving of the present blind worship accorded them. Scientists slowly became unable to think clearly because of new complexes developed while attacking the most absurd and blatant superstitions. Eventually the logical dogma of nothing really supernatural when once understood changed to nothing exists but the physical elements: matter, force, time and space. This dogma was a disaster to the human race. In its wake came the extending of the new dogma to its logical extreme and the resulting blanket denial of any intelligence lying beyond the created universe. The universe was now looked upon as a machine which accidentally happened to create itself as if built by a superior intelligence. It was accepted as such and considered logically - again, once the creator had been away with - to be a machine running itself without an engineer or consciousness back of it."

- Max Freedom Long

Obscuratus est Sol et Aer

"Only in your self can darkness exist. You pray for a devil that does not exist. You pray for a darkness that does not toil against you. You feel that where there is light there must also be darkness. It is you who fights against yourself, and is it not said that a house divided against itself cannot stand? You, who stand against the light, so that your own duplicity can contain darkness, you keep your self from the very light you crave. You jump from shadows for fear of what cannot exist, you personify evil so that you can feel comfortable in your faith, you ask for salvation from a scapegoat you stand against. Do you not see your own mistake? Open your eyes, oh Saint of Creation. You are drunk on your own philosophy."

For you who seek evil in everything, you will find it . Whatever the mind obsesses upon, it will see it everywhere. Eventually, nothing will go unpainted by your brush, nothing will go untainted by your impure vision, and even children in their natural purity will become abominations before you. For even the devil has something to teach, and is neither your enemy nor your friend. Nothing is so, except as the mind makes it so.

God has given you a divine insight, the reflection of god in you is as the reflection of the author in the character, the artist in the painting, and the architect in the building. God is within everything: God is in both goodness and evil. God has given you neither dogma nor does God regulate your life. God has not given you knowledge, but theory. God has given you enough inspiration to find God in everything, and as everything becomes painted by that brush, nothing will remain unholy, for even Death must become Birth, Illusion will become revealed, Obscurity will become Clarified, and the Darkness will become Light. Nothing is so except as the mind makes it so.

Fragment

"To Perfect Oneself, To Enlighten Mankind, To Heal and Steward the Environment."

There are no higher ideals.

As the first age of the Society has resolved itself to oblivion, we have determined that it is time to clear the slate and determine, in an exact measure, the nature of the universe in a profound and absolute manner: The human may only experience the universe in a very empirical and scientific manner, which looks without to see the reflection of what is within. This beatific language describes a simple notion, that the universe is a symbolic model, an illusion created by the mind to model and then manipulate the macrocosm.

Such large words are easily lost on the mundane seeker, who is generally unaware of the light, as manifest reality is much easier to navigate and to operate within. There are rules which guide and cannot easily be broken, and these create the limitations of our environment.

Invocat

"We cannot run from who we are, our destiny chooses us." As interesting a philosophy as this is, it is far too arbitrary for most people to understand with a simple material evaluation of their lives. What is this destiny, and how does it make choices for our lives? What is this mystical "path" that we must follow in order to be true to ourselves? Many such questions along this line of inquiry rarely ever pass into the minds of most people, and when these lines are crossed, most will give in to the unsolved equation, unwilling, unable, or simply unimpressed by the inner revelations contained in the answers.

Far to common is it that the human mind, unable to comprehend the immaterial, intangible universe that we try to find a peace of mind in material reality. We are unable to communicate our inner awareness to others effectively, and so give up in frustration. Consequently, it is not the loss to others, but a loss to ourselves that is the greatest of tragedies when unreconciled questions remain in the mind.

Over a century ago, the commoner was still held in awe over the concepts held within religion and philosophy. Now we are unconcerned, thinking our own personal philosophy: uneducated and unevolved past a hatchling of a simple thought that we far too often decide to blind and deafen ourselves to the intellect, and pursue more tangible material matters. Family, society, materialism, and career consumer our imaginations, reality becomes simple existence, in other words, the existence of the simple minded. There is honor in fulfilling social roles, but where does this lead to a greater intelligence? Where can this lead to a greater evolution for humanity? A selfish consideration of most people is that there is no more to the mind than a brain, no more to imagination than a daydream, and no more to magic than a deck of cards and a few tricks. That kind of ignorance is typical, and unfortunately, below a species so provided with such potential.

Where does the intellect fit in this effete world of consumer driven entertainment and propaganda? We are told how to think, so that we are better controlled, so that those in control can retain a sense of importance and power.

The Seed of the Heart

The Doctrine suggests that the universe is Maya, or illusion. The mystic realizes that this is so because the experience of the universe is only possible through one's own senses, and the data received from these senses is developed by our minds into a model that we call "reality". This "reality" is completely subjective and is also modified by interpretation, opinion, and belief.

"Scientific statistics will not gauge "Laziness", and would only hypothesize that some brain chemistry is at fault. Though brain chemistry may be affected through ones behavior, it is not the reason why behaviors become repetitive. This is called "Associative Conditioning", proven by Ivan Pavlov's methods.

"Following this change in perception is the changing in behavior through introspection and self evaluation. This requires the ability to perceive a model of what the person wishes to become – a self-created role model. In history this has been any sort of Hero, Deity, God, &c. We have a tendency to desire what belongs to others, and thus give up our True Will for the illusion of satisfaction. In fact, we identify ourselves through our associations with those things in our environment. To avoid this pitfall, the magician has devised a spiritual role model called the "Perfected Self". This is similar to the "Higher Self" or the "Holy Guardian Angel". The Perfected Self is yourself in the distant (or not so distant) future, the perfect and enlightened "you" that is in the process of becoming. This is ultimately the goal of every soul, to attain this level of illumination. This is the highest Order that humanity can attain to and still remain human. It is the complete realization of the Divinity within. Many people have called this the "Conversation with the Holy Guardian Angel", but "Conversion with the Perfected Self" would describe our method much more effectively.

"Because this Perfected Self is perfectly Illumined, it is beyond all temptation, beyond all Ego, and beyond all forms of obscurity that mankind is heir to. This BE-ing is beyond space and time, beyond limitation. It is as perfect as God, but still only a child of God, not yet itself a God, lacking still the ability to maintain a macrocosm outside of itself. It has moved beyond all desire and into a perception of pure Holiness.

"The Invocation of this Perfected Self is much more desirable than the Invocation of God, as God is so much more than we as limited creatures can imagine. Every "vision" of God has its limitations in the imagination faculties of man. We are presently imperfect, and thus have not the capability to comprehend God in IT's limitlessness. "There are more things in heaven and earth, Horatio, than are dreamt of in your philosophy." (Ibid.) God is pure, undifferentiated Be-ing, and cannot be accurately described as anything else. (In this is the secret of all cosmologies and dogmas proven false. Every "Law" of God is a law of man, having no relation to God's Will except through Religion (discipline, restraint, institutionalized conformity).

"The invocation of this Perfected Self draws us towards it, creating within us a union of divine force with our conscious reality. We move from Unconscious Incompetence (that is, inability to perceive the Divinity within ourselves, ignorance), to Conscious Incompetence (the ability to recognize our imperfection, and yearn towards that divine state), to Conscious Competence (the utilization of the Methods of Invocation to bring one towards Illumination), and finally to Unconscious Competence (where we have attained the Siddhas and have begun conversion with our Perfected Selves to the point where we are becoming so much more than what is commonly accepted as "Human", where our aspiration to Realizing our own Divinity takes form in our behaviors and Illumination).

"This Perfected self cannot be tainted by our Invocation, as it has itself moved beyond limitation. We in turn purify and initiate ourselves through consistent and repetitive practice of the invocation. This is where "Touch and be touched" no longer applies to the magician who has moved outside of the common destiny of mankind. We are no longer, thus, ruled by the stars, no longer subject to another person's Will, no longer controlled by our habitual and conditioned behaviors. We become fully aware every moment, exhibiting the attainment of perfect Dharma and Presence. This attainment and the fulfillment of one's Role as an Illuminated Be-ing is the True Will spoken of by so many, who themselves little understood the concept."

A meaningful spirituality in a modern world

In the closing half of the twentieth century, and the opening half of the twenty first, we are renewing our efforts towards healing the world and taking a more spiritual path. People are seeing, as if for the first time the relevance of their actions upon the planet, and are realizing their impact upon it as individuals. People are awakening to the atrocities committed by their governments, their clergy and other authority figures. People are noticing that when they make a mess they often cannot clean it up in time to save millions of lives, animal, plant and human. People are stumbling, rather forcefully into enlightenment, and many are becoming lost because of a standard that seems to mean less and less each day. Freedom is no longer considered "Free", but carries a hidden cost and a bargain value which must be paid in blood.

In this age of awakening idealism and struggling altruism, we are beginning to realize that our religious connections are becoming less and less significant as we start to understand that the teachings are intolerant and prejudiced. In this renewal of interest in our mystical roots, we are beginning to realize that the time has come for us to seek a much more practical, meaningful spirituality. The ascetic religions of our ancestors are no longer acceptable to an awakening society, who would rather seek a mysticism which enhances their experience of reality, rather than surrendering their experiences to abstinence. These ages of ignorance are coming to a close, and the age of enlightenment is at hand. This is a time when the inner doctrines and secret teachings of our traditions become unrestricted, and the commoner may study in depth the lessons once kept only for students of the occult.

The traditions of Kabbalah and Yoga combined with the practical modeling methods of Neuro-Lingustic Programming

77

become most significant here. They deal with the world of psychology, archetypes, and magic which, when practiced effectively, may result in outer manifestation and materialization of the perfected self we all seek to become. We therefore have practical teachings which emphasize the formation and the elimination of suffering, the laws of creation and manifestation, and the modeling the genius of the psyche.

The current controversy in occult circles is whether the time has come for the general population to be brought into these teachings. Though this debate continues, it suffices to say that these are powerful concepts. These ideas are vital to the world in which we now live, especially in light of the recent tragedies around the world. The time has come that we risk more if we do not study these spiritual disciplines. The time has come when we must share them; when these practices are combined they go far beyond the rigidity of traditional dogma and become a contagion of enlightenment. The time has come for us all to understand the workings of the unseen world in a way that is practical and that helps make real change in the way we exist.

Ultimately, the meticulous map of the unseen world that is provided by the Kabbalistic, Yogic and Neuro Linguistic principles have the potential to teach us about psychological, and spiritual illumination. They bring new meaning, depth and spiritual light to a world filled with suffering, ignorance and the darkness of delusion, since within these teachings are the resources for a fulfilling life.

When we discuss the distribution of these secret doctrines, we must begin at their origins. Religion grew out of the need for hope, the crutch built on fear. Practical occultism is the applied and creative destruction of both hope and fear, as both are unnecessary to the perfected being. Suffering is developed in conflict and all the problems experienced in life, including those within the mind. Suffering is the condition of stress and frustration. Religion has been mankind's search for the source of suffering: a scapegoat.

As far as humanity could see, all difficulty in human society was directed by people. In the social order, man was the controller, but the natural world was beyond man's control. Still, humanity concluded that there must be someone directing things, so he searched for this supernatural being, the source of all natural forces. These were the deities that brought the earthquakes, the floods, the fires and the storm winds. This is the emergence of religion. Observing that in human society there are leaders who exercise reward and punishment, they applied this same model to the forces behind nature. Thus, freedom from suffering had to be sought from its source, supernatural deities. The results were diverse techniques and ceremonies for showing respect, paying homage, sacrifices, prayer, etc. The Will of these deities became the constructive or destructive cause behind every event in the world.

Suffering is a natural process which must be understood in order to be controlled, and it works according to the most fundamental laws of karma. Ignorance of the laws of karma are the cause of suffering. The remedy for difficulty is wisdom, reason, knowledge and understanding.

The work of correcting the factors involved in the creation of suffering is a human responsibility, and it is within human potential to do so. Therefore emphasis for solving the problem has shifted from the will of a supernatural force to human endeavour.

Advocatus Diaboli ("Advocate of the Devil" or "Devil's Advocate") - A popular title given to one of the most important officers of the Sacred Congregation of Rites, established in 1587, by Sixtus V, to deal juridically with processes of beatification and canonization. His official title is Promoter of the Faith

(Promotor Fidei). His duty requires him to prepare in writing all possible arguments, even at times seemingly slight, against the raising of any one to the honours of the altar. *From the Catholic Encyclopedia, copyright © 1913 by the Encyclopedia Press, Inc.*

"We cannot expect people to have respect for law and order until we teach respect to those we teach respect to those we have entrusted to enforce those laws." – Hunter S. Thompson

The Democratic system of the West promotes the idea that each person's vote counts, and that the majority rules. This system also takes for granted that the majority may be both educated and intellectually developed enough to decide for itself.

A "Majority Vote" of 50-percent-plus-or-minus-one must be viewed as anything but the "Will of the People?" With regard to any election where people are divided and/or indecisive and cannot make a legitimate unanimous decision, there is no "will" expressed, no mandate, no demand for the program one of the two candidates put forward, and no particular legitimacy for whichever contender emerges with the prize of the title "Temporary Dictator". If anything, the will of the people is for these barely competent scions of second-rate political power families to go away and stop reminding us how degraded politics has become. One of the candidates will assume office and gain access to the levers of power. But in a very real sense, it is more accurate to say that the candidates lost. Neither ignited much excitement, admiration or loyalty. Anything less than a unanimous vote shows disloyalty and ineptitude where both the system and the electorates are concerned.

Similarly, it is expected that the "Average" person is capable of educating and rearing a child in the modern world, and yet it requires a PhD degree in order to operate on a person's psychology, usually damaged from common misconceptions and inept parenting.

Under ideal Socialist conditions, every person is both educated and healthy, but still able to rise above an ever emergent "average" majority. The concept of personal development and perfection of self is still in the premature stages of development, and until such a time as the "average" person rises above traumatic and instable attitude of "well – adjusted" we will (as a race) remain in a dark ages.

In this democratic community, a person is considered "Sane" only as long as he or she is able to demonstrate the ability to reason and make healthy decisions, and successfully survive in modern society. And yet, this "Sane" western mentality rarely rises above the "average". One in six children is sexually abused (17%), one in four children is physically abused (25%), eight in ten children is verbally or emotionally abused (80%), 35% of Americans over the age of 13 smoke cigarettes, &c. ... the list goes on and on. In this democratic community, a person is considered "Sane" only as long as he or she is able to pay taxes, and if he or she fails in that duty, it is a criminal offence, not a mental inadequacy.

"We cannot expect people to have respect for law and order until we teach respect to those we have entrusted to enforce those laws. " – Hunter S. Thompson

Passages

It has been the distraction of the human mind to meditate upon the Uncreated, to attempt to acquire a great reputation for depth and breadth of thought. Do they serve a God of their own making; venerating and praising the things of Heaven? Eventually the worshippers have feasted enough.

Whose names have changed into those of archaic divinities of which the normal mind is only a reflection? We can argue that this does not qualify our hallucination as a candidate for "Savior", but Sunday drags the disciple from her home in prostration and prayer.

Awakening

Kindness is ignored,
and looked upon as weakness.
Where there is no mercy in the heart of the nations,
there is no mercy in the heart of the individual.
Where hate and scorn rule the mind,
so too must pain and fear rule the soul.
And for these numb to divinity,
I pray forgiveness.
For these deprived of holiness,
I pray awareness.
One day mankind will awaken,
one day, very, very soon.
Insha'allah

This poem answers one I received from a friend on terrorism and
the human ability to ignore a call to global action..."What can I
do? I'm only one person."...and the answer is so simple:
Democracy is a unanimous vote of all those who cared to.

Automata

It has been forty days since the inception of the experiment. Today is a grand day. Today I awoke with the scent of Espresso Creama in the morning air. No other willing participants in this experiment. The cost is too great for them to mistake the information, the consequences far too long reaching if I am right. But who would know? Who would understand the dataset? The material? The proofs?

I have been called a mystic when I wished to be called a philosopher. I have been mistyped "Artist" in place of "Scientist". The information is not hard to understand. It is just far too dry for the ordinary mind. Can you feel the surface of your brain corroding under the arid winds of my Hypothesis? But then, I couldn't expect you to understand. They may find this manuscript three hundred years from now and call it the bible. Religions will arise from the false notions of the old. I shun your religion, as it is neither Holy nor True. It falls away in the face of temptation. It becomes Heresy to those who are too weak in the mind to tolerate humble honesty.

I have multiple personalities. Not in the way of normal possessed beings, but in the manner of character. Frater This, Soror That, Society of the Whatever. The interesting thing is, the subject matter is an illusion with a structure of tangible symbol systems and representations of mathematical and psychological realities. It is a system of Metaphors, designed exclusively to develop the mind, to conquer the soul.

There are not enough hours in the day. I am awakened by the light of dawn, sun rising over the windowsill above the mountain peaks across the morning British Columbia mists. Yoga in the morning with my wife and daughters, breakfast and then work. Today is no different than any other, except the anniversary; The Saintly Fortieth Day. Temptation by demons in a world not of the world. I am no ascetic. Socialist? Perhaps, and far too fond of a capitalist society to be of use in a Marxist universe.

The computer is my laboratory. The Mind of the Mystic is my data-set. Mysticism, that word of many meanings, but the only one that counts is as difficult to realize completely as the Perfection of Self that its mastery promises. A lifetime of dedication, and forty days of dedicated practice. Ritual is my programming. The paraphernalia of my art a series of binary codes developed to represent the Kabalistic and Archetypal formulae. I prepare for the experiment every morning with the same Invocation that every Mystic has memorized. The words and languages may differ, the symbols are as subjective as the perceptions we use to understand them with. I have become lost in their context, subdued by their intricate matrix of allegory and imagery.

"...Among the garbage and the Flowers..." whispers the Lion Priest, Leonard Cohen. The Garbage and the Flowers: another metaphor, another symbol. Mysticism is everywhere. Some of you might call it language. But this one line, this simple phrase carries volumes of surreptitious information. In fact, many influential thinkers have looked at such patterns among symbols. Some of our most ancient writings suggest that the original Hebrew characters and their positions within the two-dimensional array of the page reveals new meaning in every phrase.

The letters upon the pages are numbers in an ancient dialect, revealing the truth that each concept, each idea has a value. Each word is a number intimately related to every other mathematical formula sharing that number. Cross reference and indexing each one with a line of code, zeros and ones blur past my eyes. The Silent Aleph, One. Not such a vulgar system as numerology, but a definitive series of significant meaning alluding to all other meanings. Exact references, using the human ability to bind together two entirely unrelated concepts with the cord of revelation.

```
…VAR <0I000I>:
GOTO H:/Alephbet/17/
WRITE < Chet >: …
```

The letters of the alephbet are the causal link between the Tree of Life and the Tree of the Knowledge of Good and Evil. To the degree we perceive language to be primarily denotative and rooted in the tangible things of this world, we partake of the lesser tree. To the degree we perceive the connotative and transforming dimensions of language by its use of allusion to the principles underlying creation, we are partaking of the higher tree that leads to life eternal.

The hour strikes and the sun splashes across the South facing window pane, glistening flowers of light shower my desk, announcing noon. I arise from my desk and stretch, noticing the crisp edges of each and every object, examining the aura around the circumference as a light of the true nature of the universe: energy and life force. Even my computer glows with a mysterious white outline, reflecting that my eyes are not the only sense with which I see.

"Hekas, Hekas, Este Bebeloi!" We announce over our food, as is the tradition in our home. This series followed by our thanksgiving: not to a nameless God, but to recognize that the experience of appreciation banishes all pessimism.

Meditation of two hours. It is the maintenance of complete awareness in the absence of stimulation. It is the cultivation of perfect alertness of mind and control over the subtleties of being. Not a "Turning off" of the mind, but an organization so thorough that every thought is completely accounted for, every movement ruled by mastery of the flesh. Every breath inhaled for thirty seconds, held for thirty seconds, released for thirty seconds, withheld for thirty seconds, each in a complete cyclical breath through the chakras in the electrical body and the arteries of the physical.

The afternoon's work is a blur of alephbetic correspondences and codex …the sacred scripture of the Torah Shebiksav and the Torah Sheb'al Peh. Numbers and letters combined to create ideas, concentrated in a tangle of interrelated structure and meaning. There are no impure ideas here. This days work is only of the greatest accuracy and truth. Tomorrow, perhaps, I may choose otherwise, but today is a day of Adonijah.

The mountain air blows crisp against my face, the standing meditation against the banks of the cold mountain lake. The Hindus called this Vrkshasana, the Tree Pose. I am held upright by a network of roots that spreads out and pulls downward. I am grounded by a network of branches which pull me down into the ground. As the moon follows the sun, so too does my mind follow the serenity of the tree.

The sky darkens and the feast awaits. Dinner is light, and the vegetables are fresh from our garden. Excepting our prayers, there has been no talking, no garrulous and empty speech, only loving appreciation. Today is an auspicious day.

Ah, for you who would misplace the ideas and ideologies of religion thinking them severe and abstinent do not understand the true meaning of the word. As I make love to my wife in the darkness of our room I can see her form silhouette against the moonlight, a faint blue glow surrounding us as our auras intertwine, the atmosphere crackling with a static charge. Our minds are focused on experiencing each other, and the divinity within each of us becomes one as we build and release. Oh, for you who would forget that God is Love, I pity all that you have failed to perceive! In this I have found that all-loving, all-encompassing Universal Intelligence within us all. God is not in your buildings of wood and stone. Thou art God, and in this there is only one true, acceptable, and finally ultimate goal for each soul - Divinity and Human Perfection. In our union we create God, we make God, just as we would make Love.

And even here there is science. Even here there are universal codes hidden within the moans and whispers. There are frequencies of sounds, there are vibrations and octaves. They all have a mathematical key, and can relate by this to Euclidian logic and Pythagorean Mysticism. The Hebrew Language is Mathematics, and every sound is a creature. Berashit ... In the Beginning. Could you possibly understand with your vulgar mind that God is a Verb? All Infinite Be-ing. God is within you and all around you; the Rabbit and the Wolf; the hunter and the hunted; the stalker and the prey. "Each number in infinite. There is no difference."

Desktop Magician

Consistency Heuristic, educated guesses and unknown properties. Gifted children addicted to the glowing screen, where one's needs can only be gratified through communication with a pseudonymned outside world. And mine eyes I dare not open, because of the foulness of the vision.

Eliminate non-zero neuron thresholds, the tempo quickening, the music eating through the skin, mixing with the nerves and small veins. The poets have feigned songs, and the prophets speak vain things, and young men type immaculately. I cannot bear the vision!

Force specialization on the most general model. The mere manipulation may be reinforcing enough to keep the average from deteriorating too quickly. A Christ crucified, not upon Calvary, but upon the barren screens of the Internet.

Perfection of self through ritual and meditation. Gifted children addicted to the glowing screen, contemplating suspect information. Observe the impact of this unregenerate sloth!

The White Baboon

Answer to Jo Goodwin Parker's "What is Poverty"

I am experienced in recognizing the psychology of the poor. I know the vacant expressions of those who have lost hope and have traded their aspirations for humiliation. I have watched close friends pawn their bodies to feed the crutch of their addictions. I know that there is escape from destitution, for I have supported my ambition with creativity, resourcefulness, and most important of all, persistence.

Jo Goodwin Parker, in her essay entitled "What is Poverty?" writes, "Look at us with an angry heart, anger that will help you help me." I can relate to her indigence, but it is her prison of inertia which invokes my anger. Her inability to act in spite of her humiliation drives my anger. She adds, "Others like me are all around you", and this further fuels my indignation.

I have experienced the same impoverishment that Ms. Parker describes: the cutting smell of urine and sour milk, cold baths with acrid soap, 'friendly' neighbors content to neglect or abuse my sister and I while our mother was away. I know all too well that poverty is, "cooking without food and cleaning without soap", but I was able to use the discarded stub of a pencil to write my first poem. I was able to dig in the trashcans for bottles and unwanted treasures to sell. I looked for opportunity, even when it took the form of charitable alms of food and clothing. The poor may not have money, but they do have a fortune in time: time to master skills, time to write, paint, or sculpt — even when the pencil is a dull nub, the paint is made from egg whites and tea, and the sculpture is cast from mud.

Resourcefulness is not an option for Ms. Parker, who justifies her lack of ambition with the "acid that drips on pride until pride is worn away" and the "chisel that chips on honor until honor is worn away." She can "dream of a time when there is money", but has overlooked the time to make money from her dreams.

When we are born, we have no cloths, no possessions, and are ignorant of the judgment and criticism of others. When we die, we return to this natural human condition, taking little comfort in valueless material objects, and finding no humiliation in judgment and criticism. Poverty is this natural state, bereft of social value and material comforts. We are supplied with creativity, resourcefulness, and persistence of action. Every animal is afforded these, and those that do not must rely on the charity of others to provide them. Ms. Parker has no faith in persistence, instead choosing to believe in despotism, defeat and despair. She asks if we could persist year after year. In reply, the late President of the United States, Calvin Coolidge is quoted as saying:

> "Nothing in the world can take the place of persistence. Talent will not; nothing is more common than unsuccessful men with talent. Genius will not; unrewarded genius is almost a proverb. Education will not; the world is full of educated derelicts. Persistence and determination alone are omnipotent."

The poor may be without education, employment, or the luxuries which are commonplace for many of us, but they do have the most important qualities inherent in every human being. These are the intangible assets that each one of us has, regardless of our station or qualifications. The ability to create, to exploit opportunities, to take action and to persist until a goal is reached are the wealth of mankind. There is nothing more valuable than these, except the omnipotent power of sentience to put them to use. Ms. Parker asks, "What is poverty?" My answer is that Poverty is the ability to rise above the natural human condition through creative, resourceful, and persistent action.

Samizdat

sa•miz•dat: Pronunciation: 'sä-mEz-"dät; Function: noun; Etymology: Russian, from sam- self- + izdatel'stvo publishing house; Date: 1967: a system in the U.S.S.R. and countries within its orbit by which government-suppressed literature was clandestinely printed and distributed; also: such literature; also synonymous with "self-publishing". (Marriam-Webster)

In the world of internet publication, from personal web journals to corporate financial statements, each person has the ability to share uncensored ideas and communicate freely with the world for the very first time. The advances in desktop publishing allow the writer, photographer, artist and poet to print and share their work in a manner never before thought possible, as any person with access to a computer or Xerox machine may produce and print a manuscript. To undertake a self-published project, each aspiring writer must begin to understand that anyone may produce a book, that publishing is not only the domain of large commercial publishers, and what considerations may be necessary to prepare the finished product for retail outlets.

Everybody, regardless of their education, ethnic background, and culture has a subject that they are knowledgeable or passionate about. People do not have to be talented writers to share information; they must only have the desire to communicate what they know with others. Many potential publishers have subscribed to the "starving artist" belief system, often overlooking the modern ability to manufacture their work in different formats and mediums. Many people believe that genius is required to become a well known writer or artist, but forget that Walter Disney didn't know how to draw, Ani Defranco didn't know how to sing, and William Wordsworth didn't know how to write. What sets these famous names apart from the unpublished and unknown is their wish to share their passion with others, and their willingness to publish their own work. The variety of literature, art, and information is endless, and the ability to share them with others is now accessible to nearly everyone in the Western world.

For too long have writers believed that, in order to be published they must submit their writing to established commercial publishing companies, and that only the best manuscripts are chosen to be printed. The reality is that publishing is a business, and profit is the fundamental purpose of all commercial projects. Publishers do not take risks, and often only publish for established, credible writers. Publishing houses must follow trends, and will regularly ignore otherwise good writing for popular topics. Bill Henderson, editor of "The Publish It Yourself Handbook", comments that, "Commercial [publishing] houses seldom take a chance on a book unless it promises to show a profit." Marion Crook, co-author of the self-published work "How to Self Publish and Make Money" agrees, stating that, "Large publishing houses have strong commercial reasons for publishing: the book must appeal to many people, it must reflect the current social values, [and] it must be promotable."

A self-published writer must be willing to compile, edit, proofread, print, market and distribute the work by themselves. Foster J. Dickson, Production Manager for New South Books, says, "I tell people often -- and I believe it -- that writing is about art and publication is about money." He further warns future self-publishers of vanity publishing companies, who will often only succeed at separating a writer from their money. He recommends that the future publisher obtain as many quotes from printing companies and "print on demand" agencies, and have a lawyer or literary agent look over the contracts before authorizing them.

Presently, the price of manufacturing a two hundred page soft-cover book at your local Xeroxing copy company, at ten cents a sheet is approximately $7.00 in Canada if you include binding and a laminated color cover. Vanity publishers offer a price anywhere from $4.00 to $25.00+, depending upon the services offered. Many medium sized printing companies will produce a book for approximately $10.00, depending upon the size of the order and the variations in format and quality. A limited leather bound edition with hand-made silk-bond paper will certainly run over $250.00 to produce, but the author may also be able to sell the edition for well over four times that number to serious collectors, if the content reasonably matches the exterior, but this is not really economical to the small-press publisher.

Considerations which often confuse the novice publisher are ISBN numbers, UPC codes, and Copyrights. The ISBN, or International Standard Book Number, is a universal book numbering system. The National Library of Canada webpage adds that, "...by assigning a unique ten-digit number to each published title, the system provides that title with its own, unduplicated, internationally recognized identity." The price of an ISBN number from the National Library is approximately $25.00, but a minimum block of ten must be purchased. When an ISBN number is issued by the National Library of Canada, two copies are requested for their archives. (National Library of Canada) Although registering the ISBN is not necessary to privately publish a book, most bookstores use the number to catalogue the titles they carry, and will not carry a book without it. Many larger bookstores also require UPC, or Universal Product Codes, which help them to track inventory and reorder merchandise, but this is not necessary for the small publisher, as most bookstores also have the ability to create their own directly from a computer program. If a UPC code is used, the most common is the "EAN-Bookland" format, which includes a Price Code, the ISBN number, and a separate code for the Currency used, such as Canadian or US dollars. Every work is automatically copy written at the moment of its creation, and permission must be used in order for anyone to make a copy of the material. Copyrights in Canada are free and automatic, but legal verification may be required if the ownership of a work is ever called into question. The most convenient way to do this is to have a copy sealed in an envelope by a Commissioner of Oaths and placed in a safety deposit box, where it will remain indefinitely as evidence.

Self-Publishing has a long history if innovation and invention. It has been the driving force of political movements, campaigns of propaganda, and the voice of the people since literacy became common amongst the world's citizens. In the eras of fascism and totalitarianism, Samizdat exists parallel to officially sanctioned printing and publishing, creating literature that has not been subjected to censorship. Publishing has weathered political and religious domination, and has revealed fantastic worlds of fiction and imagination. Great poetry has been written and self-published by small press publishers, and will continue to play a great part in the fashioning of human intelligence.

Works Cited:

The Marriam-Webster Online Dictionary. 24 Nov, 2003.

Signposts: A Guide to Self-Publishing. 29 Nov, 2003

Dickson, Foster J. The Tricky Art of Self-Publishing. The Writer's Resource Center. 29 Nov, 2003. < http://www.poewar.com/articles/selfpublishing.htm>

The National Library of Canada, 30 Nov, 2003

Henderson, Bill. The Publish It Yourself Handbook: Literary Tradition and How-To. Yonkers, N.Y. :Pushcart Book Press, 1973.

Wise, Nancy and Crook, Marion. How to Self Publish and Make Money. Kelowna, British Columbia: Sandhilll Book Marketing Ltd., 1997

Temple Invocation
of the Sub-Elementals

The following is a Cut Up poem, a form of "word collage". I know many of you might understand what this might be, but I thought I'd give a brief introduction to those who don't. A "Cut Up" is a random selection of quotes spliced together to form a coherent poem or story. It was a favorite of Brion Gysin (close friend of Allen Ginsburg and William Burroughs). I clean mine up a bit, adding neccessary elements to have them fit a particular format. They tend to fit a pretty interesting pattern, and often have a synchronous coherancy. Let me know what you think. This particular one will be published by Octavia Publishing this month.

I invoke you, the vision and ecstasy of universal intelligence; you, who are acquainted with the secret of the harmony of Life; you, whose intimacy is a rose of divine truth! You, whose lips glow with the touch of divine prayer! O Prince of the Chariots of the Winds.

I invoke you, Citadel of universal and true Faith; you, who exists as a voice of rushing fire; you, who speaks with a thousand whirling winds; for whom wisdom is a universe unto itself, O Lord of Winds and Breezes.

I invoke you, who is a dark and stormy sea of understanding; you, for whom an impression is a complete world; the light of your thought makes clear whatever is obscure, and on your lips is the key to all sacred mysteries, O Queen of the Throne of Air.

I invoke you, whose wisdom is beyond my understanding, you, who brightens the glass of perception; I am humbled by your look, which turns dust into flames, for you kindle knowledge with the spark of Divine Love, O Princess of the Rushing Winds.

I invoke you, the soul in the body of the universe; you, who breathes music into the Light of Life; Life envies Death when death is for your sake! I have nourished your flame in my heart, O Prince of the Chariot of Fire.

I invoke you, the flame of Gnosis; you, who burns to ashes the Shroud of Ignorance; you, who demands its sacrifice in the name of Wisdom. We are dispersed like stars in the world, O Lord of Flame and Lightning.

I invoke you, whose blaze enthrones the sun in the sky, and lightning encircles you with adoration for ever; give us the sleepless eye and the passionate heart; be the mirror of mine all-burning love, O Queen of the Thrones of Fire.

I invoke you, idol image fired into my mind. I seek the secrets within my Soul. I seek the mysteries of my nature. Once more dwell in our breasts, O Princess of the Shining Flame.

I invoke you, protector of the Light of the universe; you, who has filled our glass with the sweet wine of knowledge. The Sun and Moon are bright with your radiance. You have washed from me self conceit and arrogance, O Prince of the Chariot of the Waves.

I invoke you, oh prison guard of my own mind; you, who have broken loose the wheel of time; you, who acknowledges neither beginning nor end, whose thought is eternal, whose gift is infinitude, O Lord of Waves and the Waters

I invoke you, the conscience hidden in God's heart; you, in whose essence divinity is mirrored. In your womb is built a new world of true Be-ing! You have graced our minds with the gnosis of truth, O Queen of the Thrones of the Water.

I invoke you, the bright radiance of God's eye; you, who knows that the Sun does not last forever, for who joy and sorrow are nothing; you, who showers with Light the gardens of Life, O Princess of the Waters.

I invoke you, the Heart of Honor and the Glory of Love; you, who causes the beams of true spiritual Light to shine; you, whose spread lips broke the silence with ecstatic utterance; the great Being who holds influence over sun, moon, and stars, O Prince of the Chariot of Earth.

I invoke you, the Fearless Thought which passes beyond Heaven; you, who reconciles Lifelessness with Immortality; you, who fan the Flames of Life with the breath of Gnosis; your perfect understanding and illumination is the Heart of the Mind, O Lord of the Wild and Fertile Land.

I invoke you, who is the Holy Water of Life; you, who are the Womb of the Earth, regarding yourself as both the clay and the water; you, the granite which floats and the moisture which sinks. Where, in those places where the Sun cannot reach, Darkness is known by another name, O Queen of the Thrones of Earth.

I invoke you, O Gate of Truth and Darkness Illuminated; you, who is the Ashes of Existence and Life in Death, for whom the stars keep lit and for whom the Sun rises; the Black Stone becomes a mind of Clearest Diamond, O Princess of Echoing Hills.

"There are many events in the womb of time which will be delivered upon you. An intelligent man is observant of spirit, but a wiser man is observant of his ear, and perceives the serpent's tongue where it is most likely to cause a vulgar thought." – Frater Ego Esse

Apostate

The flame burns within and without,
The scars form writhes within living flesh,
The burn sears the name from my mind.

I hear you reply with a broken mirror voice
That my tragedy is my own misplaced ambition,
And my only wealth is aimless frustration.

I watch you with a decade long stare,
I revere my hero with subtle distaste,
The masochistic worship empty with blindness.

Oh Christ, your savior, has proven remote.
YHVH is a delinquent father, a savage reminder
That you could not be worthy of better company.

Friendship to you is an empty excuse
To burn, scar, and eventually abandon.
An opponent bereft of form: any name will do.

I could not save you, but took sick comfort
In watching you destroy yourself.
I abhor your friendship, and despise your influence.

To become a martyr of your own misery
Within my dirty remembrance of you
Is exactly what you would desire.

I know your secrets, pitiful to the trained eye:
You attack with a question, which has no answer,
And sneer at the jointly fallen opponent.

My dear mentor, you have no answers of your own,
Only quick, medicated explanations,

Which leaves your bitter soul beneath.

Only with a strange reminiscence do I look back,
And spit on the blackened earth which remains
For you are more than a memory, and less than a man.

Objectivity in Occultism

The training of the mind in a matter of any discipline requires an unprejudiced perception on the part of the occultist. We must consider that the destruction of our previously held beliefs will meet with terrible objection from the mind, and from the minds of others. It is a matter of reprogramming ourselves based on acceptance that we as common humans do not know anything except that with which we are given. Our entire lifetime we have been presented with "truth" in a myriad of forms, and have struggled to include them into our daily understanding of the universe — many of us have even chosen to reinterpret events in the light of our diseased self-identifying systems of thought. The mind will react out of sheer desperation, for we are so used to habitually reinterpreting our peceptions based on our pretext that we choose to experience the universe through a tainted lens.

The rare person, one who has no religious affiliation, nor one who has been affected by a dogma which is often interspersed with our social programming, must still conquer the perceived self. We do not initially understand that every action, every thought, is entirely controlled and controllable by the conscious person. In fact, very few people ever realize that they can control their own behaviors, their own thoughts, their own emotions, and ultimately, their own states of being. We have accepted so many false ideas that the removal of these limitations will suffer us with the fear of freedom. For the lack of a crutch, we fear we may ultimately topple over. The mind has been prepared by a limited view for most of our lives, and we are often not prepared for the new conditions within which we may live, if earnest effort is taken to become free of our deceptions and illusions. Many of us have not been made aware of poisonous thoughts and emotional rubbish. Contradictions in our behavior make for a confusing and often insane personality structure. The same person may find him or herself believing that murder is a terrible thing, but may also believe that a veteran of war is a hero worthy of reverance.

Similarly, the ignorant and superstitious may think that the cultivation of miracles is the trademark of a devil, and simultaneously worship a man who was known to carry on with many strange workings! We may live in a world of technological wonder, but forget that our house of cards may also tumble, leaving us in another dark age. Many people living now are entirely unaware of what it is to be fully human, and could not be made to care whether or not we are more than intelligent animals or not. Most humans today are primitive beasts without any real comprehension of the wrong attitudes they keep. We live in constant and imminent danger of war, starvation, crime, and cruelty in our very neighborhoods. We live in a constant state of anxiety and perpetual despair, and find comfort in the opiate of television sensationalism and mind destroying noise.

It would seem that in mankind's despondency, there is little hope of escape from the trap we have sprung upon ourselves. There are many teachers of enlightenment who have offered the opportunity of escape. There have been many people who have made the commitment to emerge from darkness and seek for the light. The few among us who have attained to the higher levels of awareness shine like beacons to those who would strive to break the chains of indolence and degeneration. These are the keepers of the concealed mystery. They do not hide the knowledge, but protect it from desecration. Those who seek devoutly, who are eager to prepare themselves for its presence, will find the doors opened wide, the garments of human lassitude cast away for the vestments of initiation. Beware, those who are impure with the seed of desperation and fear, for to them the door is tightly shut, the word is silent, until such a time as they are ready for advancement.

Vibration

All that exists does so as a form of energy, vibrating at various rates of speed. Each vibration sends out a ripple in every direction which spread outwards in an infinite direction. These waves flow through each other without destroying each other, though affecting each other subtly. Heavy tangible objects are made up of dense forms of vibration, where higher frequencies create less tangible forms, such as light and sound. There are many more forms of vibration, each subtly affecting the other, many of which we are not even aware of. Until relatively recently, we did not know of electricity, radiation, and we are still in the infant stages of understanding microwaves, radio waves, magnetic waves, among others. Each of these vibrations may be discerned in octaves, such as are found in music, and may be visualized in the color spectrum of a rainbow. As the vibrations become finer and more rapid, we are no longer keenly aware of them, such as many forms of radiation. The highest frequency we have discovered is that of thought, which, like electricity, moved at a very swift pace. Each thought is a vibration, which is discernable and measurable, and affects reality in exactly the same manner as a lower vibration might. These thoughts may also be discerned in octaves, similar to sound and color as well – each having a distinct and separate scale. Just as the high frequency waves of radiation may travel through most dense waves, so too can the waves transmitted by thought move through the lower frequencies with little change to their initial structure.

In the most ancient of primitive human species, the control and management of the dense material world became the determinant factor of survival and comfort. In later generations, mankind has had to develop an understanding of other forms of vibration, each era discovering more subtle forms, and learning how we might be affected by them, each in their turn. Thought, being one of the most subtle, affects us in many different manners – both as a form of radiation, as well as its direct and obvious affect on the inward psychology and outward behaviors of the human being. Because the human is affected by every form of vibration, would it not be safe to assume that the next degree of our evolution would be to manage and control these as well?

What sensitive people there are who can see the innumerable thought-forms and can read the thought vibrations as if they were thoughts of their own? Many thoughts develop lives of their own, creating an entity which is housed within the mind of another, and acts as a being outside of that person's personality, acting of its own accord in the non-physical realms of the highest vibrations, known by many as the astral world. The astral universe exists within, and is precisely parallel to the physical universe.

If a thought has a vibration, which science has been able to detect and is beginning to learn to manipulate, then we are able to discern that "Thought is a thing", and is more than simply an electrical current operating a switchboard in the brain. There have been experiments made in the fields of biofeedback and computer science, which has lead to the development of technology which will allow a computer to receive directions from a person, who may move a cursor on a computer screen merely by "willing" it so[1] (also)[2].

Thought Vibration

The mind has control over everything that it can understand and visualize. For example, Dr. Martin L. Rossman in an article

---

[1]McCarthy Kieren, "Boffins create thought-controlled computer", April 30, 2001, The Register Newsletter, < http://www.theregister.co.uk>, Accessed June 10, 2003.

[2]Schwartz, Andrew, "Thought-Controlled Prosthetics?", June 14, 2002, The Whitaker Foundation, http://www.whitaker.org , Accessed June 10, 2003.

"Imagery: Learning to Use the Mind's Eye[3]," described how visualization works on the physical system:

> "Visual, auditory, and tactile imagery seem to arise from the brain's cerebral cortex, the seat of higher mental functions, such as language, thinking, and problem solving [...]researchers have used a [...] technique called positron emission tomography (PET) to monitor the brain during imagery exercises, they have found that the same parts of the cerebral cortex are activated whether people imagine something or actually experience it. This suggests that picturing visual images activates the optic cortex, imagining that you are listening to music arouses the auditory cortex, and conjuring up tactile sensations stimulates the sensory cortex. Thus, vivid imagery can send a message from the cerebral cortex to the lower brain centers, including the limbic system, the emotional center of the brain. From there, the message is relayed to the endocrine system and the autonomic nervous system, which can affect a range of bodily functions, including heart rate, perspiration, and blood pressure."

Thus, it is possible for the mind to control the body, in exactly the same manner as it once created that body which it controls. Ayurvedic medicine has understood this mind/body connection for millennia – certainly long before modern science began its inquiry. Ayurvedic medicine shows that underlying the physical structure of the body's health (or lack thereof) is the structure within the mind. The brain controls the body, and every cell within it. The mind uses thought to program the body, and this programming is reflected in the outward appearance of that vehicle. The mind and the body work in conjunction with each other in an intricate system of symbiosis – the mind programming

---

[3] Rossman, Dr. Martin L, "Imagery: learning to use the mind's eye (article)", 1993, "Mind, body medicine : how to use your mind for better health", Consumer Reports Books.

the body, and the body interfacing with reality to program the mind. It is possible, then, to change the programming that one is already used to, and upgrade one's quality of thoughts to a much more effective and practical formulae.

Similarly, thought may be used to affect the universe outside of the body. Mind controls the actions of the body with conditioned behaviors, acting upon the data it receives and using the body to change and manipulate the reality it perceives. Further, thought may be used to affect the minds and behaviors of others, both through speech and through the unspoken communication of the body. Above these, though, are the subtle powers of thought over the rest of the natural world.

The Back Pages

I have strange dreams. Reflections of a past life, or perhaps the illustration of the way this life is supposed to be. I lay awake in this old hotel room, the paint peeling from the walls, the creaking bed next door, the unintentional blinking of the neon light by my window. It is all so strange and beautiful. I see the tired mirror casting extra shadows around the room, the broken prism glass showering the room with candlelight and red neon. My heart aches for…for what? I don't know. I'm missing something. I couldn't tell you what. My heart aches, my soul yearns, and I don't know why. I've been denied something, but I couldn't tell you what, or why.

I'm not particularly well educated, although I once thought that I should be. I can't hold a particularly good conversation with anyone, due to their ignorance and my anti-social introspection. They tell me I'm really smart, and I tell them to bugger off. All I have in the world is in this room. An old Remington typewriter, the 'A' key askew, the ribbon occasionally bunching. Two pairs of creased and frayed pants, t-shirt and underwear drying on the radiator. Old shoes sitting by the door, socks with holes in the heels balled up on the floor. I was never particular about appearances. My jacket is about thirty years old, and I've patched the elbows more times than I've patched up my mind. I couldn't tell you how I got to be here, dumpy hotel in some Canadian city. It doesn't matter which one.

I make thirty dollars a week writing for the Herald, and they are more than happy to not be bothered with my presence. I leave the typed sheets at the lobby desk, they leave me the cash, usually in crumpled bills. It pays the rent on this room and buys a loaf of bread and a can of milk. Occasionally I need ribbon, or repairs, and they advance me more, but rarely, and with less frequency than in my youth.

I've heard it said that the final pages of a book are usually the most redundant and unimpressive, if only because they represent the final leg of a journey. I used to tell young people, when I was little older than they, that a piece of art, whether it was poetry or a painting, was never completed; only abandoned. There are no final pages in my works, a mixed series of numbers, as chaotic as the mind of a human being, as imperfect as the consciousness which mankind uses to filter his perceptions. I used to believe myself to be Jewish, but lacked the coherence and dedication. I used to find comfort in the community that would not have me – an adopted, uncircumcised goyam, who only wished community in a race of outcasts and delinquents. There was no real connection except lonely high holy days and an affinity for kabala.

I am no Hitler, whining over spilled heritage. I have no struggle except that I am alone, and that the loneliness has become a greater comfort than human accompaniment. There is no true history. We are doomed to repeat the muddled recollections of the past, regardless of our efforts to change it. It is only the man who has shed his indolence and has chosen to move that creates change in the behavior enough to shift a position. Mankind has often become arrogant in his search to change the religious habits in his life, in order to justify greater comforts. There is no Angel within, only the Devil searching for a deeper sloth. Had I a million dollars, I would give it away. There is no greater need for me than this typewriter and whatever gin I can afford. I am not for human consumption. They would not have me, and I would have it no other way.

There was once a young man who thought to befriend me. He struggled for years to understand why I hid myself away in this hotel room, occasionally looking out of the windows to view the street below, watching the tides of fashion and parliament behavior wax and wane. Decades passed before he understood that mankind is a disease, and though I cannot find it in my nature to escape humanity through suicide, I also do not wish to join it.

I spend my afternoons looking out of the only window in the 4th Street Pub, overlooking the Avenue. It doesn't matter what the name of the place is, that's changed nearly thirty times in the last few years. It isn't a profitable venture, this place. But the beer is cheap and the service isn't so bad. No one bothers you. I write while I gaze out of the window, watching people at they conveniently ignore me.

Its interesting that, as little as I know about people, I have an affinity for writing about them. Some psychic pen-work, discovering the secrets of their hearts, the desires of their souls, the mysteries of their denials and the concerns which drive them from one day to the next. Today is definitely not a day for the newspaper's work. Looking down at the coil notebook, all I see is the cynicism which has become my decades old trademark.

"You laugh, but I know what you look like on the inside. I know what color your emotion is, what hue your sarcasm takes, what shade your deceits, what values your contrivances. I know you better than you believe you know yourself. I know what thoughts you entertain, and what desires you fantasize over. I listen to your ideas when you allow your mind to wander, and it wanders every moment. I understand the depths of your emotion, the lengths to which you will go to prove yourself worthy of respect, and the heights from which you have plummeted.

"Oh, you laugh, but I understand. I have watched you in your most private moments, when you touch yourself and wish it were someone else touching you. I have watched you as you sat, lonesome, in the dark, wishing that you were not alone, and the way you pretended to ignore it. I know that you are so deeply alone. I watch you as you do those things that you would never admit to. You think that people would judge you for your private behaviors, but you believe that theirs are any less sinful? Oh, I know you. I know your feelings, I know your emotions, I know your fantasies.

"You laugh, and I can't help but wonder how often you've had to cry for the very same reasons. No, I know that the tears aren't usually real, but I know that there is an ache in your heart, there within you, that you cannot deny. Do you believe everyone is so alone? That constant ache, the desire to be needed more than you are. The need to know that without you, one's experience of life would be worthless. You beg to know that you are important, and that you have more worth than is shown you. I can only answer you with silence."

Ah, to the back pages go the answers, the conclusions, time to tie up the loose ends. One more letter before my days end. One more editorial for the back pages, three columns before the classifieds, more an honor of good years spent than an honoured columnist. The back pages, that no one reads and fills space between the advertisements. And I'm not very good at it anymore.

"We cannot run from who we are, our destiny chooses us." As interesting a philosophy as this is, it is far too arbitrary for most people to understand with a simple material evaluation of their lives. What is this destiny, and how does it make choices for our lives? What is this mystical "path" that we must follow in order to be true to ourselves? Many such questions along this line of inquiry rarely ever pass into the minds of most people, and when these lines are crossed, most will give in to the unsolved equation, unwilling, unable, or simply unimpressed by the inner revelations contained in the answers.

Far to common is it that the human mind, unable to comprehend the immaterial, intangible universe that we try to find a peace of mind in material reality. We are unable to communicate our inner awareness to others effectively, and so give up in frustration. Consequently, it is not the loss to others, but a loss to ourselves that is the greatest of tragedies when unreconciled questions remain in the mind.

Over a century ago, the commoner was still held in awe over the concepts held within religion and philosophy. Now we are unconcerned, thinking our own personal philosophy: uneducated and unevolved past a hatchling of a simple thought that we far too often decide to blind and deafen ourselves to the intellect, and pursue more tangible material matters. Family, society, materialism, and career consume our imaginations, reality becomes simple existence, in other words, the existence of the simple minded. There is honor in fulfilling social roles, but where does this lead to a greater intelligence? Where can this lead to a greater evolution for humanity? A selfish consideration of most people is that there is no more to the mind than a brain, no more to imagination than a daydream, and no more to magic than a deck of cards and a few tricks. That kind of ignorance is typical, and unfortunately, below a species so provided with such potential.

Where does the intellect fit in this effete world of consumer driven entertainment and propaganda? We are told how to think, so that we are better controlled, so that those in control can retain a sense of importance and that we can retain a sense of comfort."

Oh, I'm tired. Sleep cannot come too soon. The moonlight settles over the neon once again, and disappears behind closed eyes, to another night of dreamless torpor.

Love

"God is Love." This statement has a depth of reality far beyond what the average person wants to know even though such knowledge is critical to the work of the perfection of self. "Whoever is without love does not know God, for God is love." [I John 4:8] True love is the totality of kindness and has no circumstance where it is conditional. Loving-kindness is the reflection of God in the actions of mankind. God by any name is love, and Love is found and returned by those who seek gnosis. To appreciate the divinity within oneself is to contemplate the attributes of love. As with any practice, this will eventually become an unconscious habit, and such habits are the seed of eternal greatness. Love gives purpose to those who pursue it's practice in all things. The attainment of perfect love is the acquisition of the greatest magick in the universe. "By their actions you will know them" – and through love is the attainment of ascension possible. Absolute perfection is necessary before one can enter the presence of God.

Everyone wants to be able to do things their own way. They want to consider their way as the right way. This is a product of egocentricity (self-centeredness). Most are not willing to accept that Loving-Kindness is the product of great wisdom and selflessness - For these, the road to enlightenment is difficult.

Love is the guide to all right action, and it is through this clear view that others are brought to perfect their own characters.

Subconscious Pranayamic Learning Method

I have known for several years a method of "Downloading" information directly into the mind by bypassing the conscious judgments and ignoring the frailties of our past "left brain" learning systems.

Recently, I discovered that the same system is available (with different window dressing, of course) as an NLP course, offered by Paul Scheele. As with every method, the semantics change, but he context remains the same.

One must remember that in order to practice something new, one must be able to see the reasoning behind the method. In downloading information, you are bypassing the judgmental consciousness, as well as the sluggish manner in which we have trained ourselves to experience the world. We speak at a slow pace, we can only keep up to seven concepts active consciously at once, and we are rarely "Awake" any more than 2% of the day. Our brains filter out much of the redundant or "Unneccessary" information to allow us to both read and process information at the same time. This does not need to be the case. You may "download" the information, and allow your subconscious mind to process it, wherein it automatically becomes a natural extension of your knowledge base. With practice, you will be able to remember the information as if it were your own genius, your own ideas coming to the surface. This is the most natural way to learn, and is how you processed information as a child.

As a child, your learned the spoken word by associating information to a concept through repetition. Similarly, you learned how to associate letters to sounds, sounds to the squiggles on the page, and eventually you learned that a particular series of squiggles was a word. According to one professor, it takes 4 milliseconds (there are one thousand milliseconds per second) for the brain to recognize and comprehend a word, but it takes significantly more than four milliseconds for the eye to move from one word to the next. We learn to read by pronouncing the word and correcting our pronunciation as we read, but even while learning to read silently (considered a practice of devil worship in ancient Europe) we still moved our lips, and often our psychology is limited by our physiology – we speak slowly, our eyes move from letter to letter slowly, and we type or write slowly.

A simplified and condensed method of speed reading shown to the author at a very young age was simple: Learn to read by the letter, then learn to read by the word, then learn to read by the sentence, and finally, learn to read by the page. Imagination is the final arbiter of the method, where intuition becomes the interface between yourself and you mind.

Subconscious Pranayamic Learning

Begin by choosing a book to read.

Meditate a moment, relaxing the mind, breathing deeply and steadily.

Open the book to the first page. Take a deep inbreath and focus on the first page, but not actually focusing on what is written there. Exhale steadily and then move on to the next page. Continue this process until the book has been completed. You may repeat this process several times (as with a dictionary or a manual), and the more you do so, the more the information is made concrete. I recommend that you then skim through the book (take about 10-15 minutes to skim through it), and you will find that you already "know" much of the information presented. Remember that repetition is the key to learning, so three or four "Downloading sessions" for a book is much more effective than only one quick scan.

With practice, and regular use of this technique, you will be able to cut study and reading time down to less than an hour to read an entire book, and with perfect comprehension of the material. In many cases (with practice), you will be able to memorize entire texts this way.

This technique is incredibly useful in learning second languages...merely pace your breathing with each word. It is possible to become fluent in an entire language within hours. (Keep in mind that you will only ever need about 200 words and phrases to "survive" in a foreign setting...and 2000-5000 words and phrases to be "Fluent" in a language, in as much as is required to carry on a conversation. The average American has a usage vocabulary of 2000 words, 70% (about 1400 words) of which are one or two syllables. A language tape which says a phrase and then repeats it in the language you are trying to learn (as well as conversational "Question/Answer" tapes) are excellent for this purpose. Breathe in with the phrase, breathe out with the translation. You might want to use this out-breathe as a vocalization.

Inspira Nobilis

Oh God, reach down and inspire man.
Man, reach up and touch divinity,
For did they not say, "Touch and be touched"?
The closer you come to perfection,
The closer to the ideal you will become.

Oh Man, reach up and become as God,
Oh God, reach down and touch humanity,
For is it not true that, "Thou art God"?
The invocation is the key to conversion,
True communication is only possible between equals.

Oh God, by what name may we know you?
Oh Man, by what word shall you call on God,
For isn't there power in the Word?
The conjuration to subtle presence,
As the servant becomes the master, finally.

Oh Mind, by what power shall we inspire you?
Ah, Body, will you become slave to the Will?
For the creature must evolve towards discipline.
Meditate upon the infinite, and nothingness.
Touch what cannot be touched, and become.

The Psychology of the Magickian

The psychology of the magickian is a simple matter to explain, but a difficult task for those ill prepared for self-knowledge.

Magick requires of its initiates a level of objective self-observation and the ability to model the thoughts and behaviors of those who have become successful in any endeavor the magickian wishes to master.

Any behavior is a learned skill, which may be mastered through confidence and determination, regardless of one's past experience. The modeling of the beliefs, physiological and psychological behaviors is imperitive to the magickian's development.

Psychology is a simple matter of communication. If you are open to understanding that your habitual thoughts and behaviors are the programming, you may inevitably control your thought patterns, physiological chemistry, and ultimately condition oneself to become aware of all available options at all times.

Magick is not a matter of "Supernatural" abilities, although they seem so to the uninitiated. Magick is the basis of manipulation of one's reality structure, which is developed through right conditioning of one's perceptions.

The perceptions are a simple matter of understanding that what we experience as reality is in fact a self created illusion. Each one of us has the ability to change what we percieve in past memory and in future responses. Our senses are created to accept data and then our minds process this data, comparing and contrasting it with past experience. This inevitably changes the information in such a way as to limit redundant information and clarify that which needs further attention. This data is corrupted by our past experiences and judgements. This data is further corrupted by our impressions and interpretations. Finally, in a universe of infinite information, our senses are designed to filter out data to prevent overwhelming sensory overload.

It is our first step as initiates to begin to control our bodies, minds and senses to process information in an effective and raw form.

What we view is not what we see.
What we listen to is not what we hear.
What we experience is not complete.

We must understand that the filters we have been using limit our experience. It is the subjective view that tells us that we are seperate individuals, created to perform specific duties and functions in a neutral and viscious universe. We become addicted to a certain biological chemistry which in itself determines our responses to certain sensations.

Our impressions limit our capacity to understand. This in turn creates a feedback loop that does not allow us further awareness, and we create a limited perception of possible behaviors. Often, we program ourselves with the minimum required actions and thus limit our possible behaviors.

It is thus the action of the initiate to awaken, to become aware of all possibilities, and not to limit any potential behaviors which might impede our abilities to experience and manipulate our environments.

7/9/3
The Elitist Opinion

My wife made a very important point to me concerning Elitist Opinion. Upon realizing that we rarely practice daily rituals and her study has been mainly focused on parenting, yoga and palmistry, rather than on magick, Hermeticism and esoteric doctrine. I failed to realize that one study in one area of practice is just as important as any other place of study. Just so, Occultism teaches that one form of worship is no more or no less important than any other form of worship.

In the same matter, she had pointed out to me that the first Obligation of the Order of the Angilluminati is "Perfection of Self", and as such, perfection of self included becoming the best parent possible. The second Obligation is "Enlightenment of Others", and becoming a great parent includes giving your children the necessary tools to become great people: wise, cunning, healthful, wealthy, intelligent, and full of loving kindness. This same perfection of self is what her magickal practices have been based on. Her feelings are very simple, and much more elite than most daily ritualists, and much more lucid: Is it wiser to practice a group of empty rituals when the few that she does practice are dedicated to the Obligation. Perhaps she does not study magick as much as I, but she does study what is important to her magickal path. One ritual done to complete gnosis, in serious contemplation, is many times more effective than a giggling schoolgirl's frenzied attempts at an LBRP. Her yogic meditations, both Asana and Astanga are many times more effective than the wandering contemplations of most pagans.

I now stand corrected: The woman is often much wiser than I am, and her wisdom in practice is much more astute than my wisdom in theory. I would be great if I were half the magickian that she is.

What is magick if one does not practice it regularly? What good are the sigils, symbols, and vibrations if one does not use them seriously towards a Will greater than ones own personal aspirations and ambitions. The Obligation of the SOTA is a simple reversal of the Magickian of the Left Hand Path: "Control of Oneself, Control of Others, Control of one's Environment", where instead our Obligation is based upon improvement for sake of enlightenment and idealistic altruism. The Obligation of the SOTA is, "Perfection of Self, Enlightenment of others, and Stewardship of the environment."

Original thoughts can be understood only in virtue of the unoriginal elements which they contain.
-- Vittorio Alfieri

www.ingramcontent.com/pod-product-compliance
Lightning Source LLC
Chambersburg PA
CBHW050412030726
47503CB00006B/2147